M000240347

FINDLAY
MARKET
—— OF ——
CINCINNATI

FINDLAY
MARKET
— OF —
CINCINNATI

A HISTORY

ALYSSA McCLANAHAN

AMERICAN PALATE

Published by American Palate
A Division of The History Press
Charleston, SC
www.historypress.com

Copyright © 2021 by Alyssa McClanahan
All rights reserved

First published 2021

ISBN 9781540250483

Library of Congress Control Number: 2021945856

Notice: The information in this book is true and complete to the best of our knowledge. It is offered without guarantee on the part of the author or The History Press. The author and The History Press disclaim all liability in connection with the use of this book.

All rights reserved. No part of this book may be reproduced or transmitted in any form whatsoever without prior written permission from the publisher except in the case of brief quotations embodied in critical articles and reviews.

CONTENTS

Acknowledgements   7
Introduction   9

1. One of Many Markets: The First Decades
   of Findlay Market   15
2. A Bustling Market: Findlay Market at the Turn
   of the Twentieth Century   46
3. Keeping Pace with the Times: The Market at Midcentury   73
4. Real Estate, Residency and Race: Findlay Market into
   the Late Twentieth Century   100
5. The Involved City: Findlay Market at the Turn of
   the Twenty-First Century   123

Epilogue. The Market Today   167
Notes   171
About the Author   189

ACKNOWLEDGEMENTS

I want to thank several archives and libraries in Cincinnati that provided invaluable resources and help. The Cincinnati Museum Center's History Library and Archives has a great number of local sources pertaining to Findlay Market. Along with other staff there, Mickey deVise' was incredibly kind, helpful and supportive. The University of Cincinnati's Blegen Library also houses many records on Cincinnati's urban history. Its head archivist, Kevin Grace, has a wealth of knowledge and was, as always, very helpful in finding collections and photos for this project. I also want to thank staff in the genealogy and local history department at the Public Library of Cincinnati and Hamilton County for their many resources related to the city's past. Librarians there, including Katrina Marshall and Christopher Smith, were very helpful with photos as well.

Ancestry.com deserves a huge thank-you. What an amazing resource for us to investigate our ancestors! Its digitized sources were essential in recovering the stories of Findlay Market's people. Time and time again, genealogy reminds me of how family stories can explain larger historical events to us in such relevant ways.

Through Ancestry, I connected with several family members of historic Findlay Market merchants. These kind individuals—including Karen Baum, Vickie Hahn, Jim Kennedy, Mary Beth Bruns, Tom Wegner, Beau and Mike Breiner and Kate Zaidan—took time to share stories and photographs with me. Thank you all.

Acknowledgements

I want to thank my acquisitions editor at The History Press, John Rodrigue, for all his work, encouragement and constant communication that went into bringing this book into being. I also want to thank History Press senior editor Ryan Finn for his work on getting this manuscript into production.

This book relies on the work of many great urban historians, too many to name here. I will mention two, though: Zane L. Miller and David Stradling. Zane is no longer with us, but he was a truly gifted historian of Cincinnati and I always learn much from reading his books. David—who is now the Zane L. Miller Professor of History at the University of Cincinnati—trained me and many others in urban history. David is an incredibly compelling writer, a great urban historian and a wonderful mentor. He taught me to care deeply about cities.

I am indebted to Mark Bruggeman, a good friend of mine and an architect who has worked on many buildings around Findlay Market. He was the one who suggested to me to write a book on Findlay Market's history. From there, Joe Hansbauer, the president of the Corporation for Findlay Market, kindly funded the initial research into this book, hoping that a better understanding of the market's past would help him direct its future better.

I want to thank my family, especially my parents, for always encouraging me and being so supportive of my endeavors.

Lastly, this book is dedicated to my partner in all things, John. He has dedicated his life so far to cities and saving their old parts.

INTRODUCTION

This is a history of Findlay Market—a historic public market in Cincinnati, Ohio—from its founding in the mid-1800s to its recent years in the early twenty-first century. But it is also a history of many places in urban America.

Findlay Market is located in Over-the-Rhine, one of three downtown neighborhoods in Cincinnati along with the West End and the central business district. Situated along the Ohio riverfront, Cincinnati's downtown basin—its urban core—is framed by the river to the south and hills to the north, east and west. The ups and downs of the market and the surrounding downtown help us to make sense of many U.S. cities and the long historical developments that shaped them. Findlay Market's history points us to moments when downtowns were healthy in the sense that they were dense and exciting, and it also reminds us of the more recent years when city centers were ill, bleeding population and losing money. Findlay Market can similarly shine a light on how integral immigrants and migrants were to U.S. cities, as well as how when you take away that cultural diversity, something is irrevocably lost. The market also reveals how racism shaped cities, denying minorities quality housing and business opportunities even as they made up the majority of residents in city centers. Finally, we can look to Findlay Market to think about how city governments shaped their cities over time, which in turn tells us a lot about how the average American saw their city— at one time, as a place to live and work; at other times, a place to flee and avoid; and now, as a place to remake.[1]

Throughout the 1800s, the United States became increasingly urbanized and industrialized, with millions moving to cities for jobs and other opportunities. Findlay Market reflected this high tide of urbanization. It started as one among many public market squares in the heart of Cincinnati, serving a fast-growing population. In the mid-1800s, when Findlay Market was founded, Cincinnati was *the* city west of the Appalachian Mountains, operating as a key commercial port and major exporter of goods. Even after Chicago and other midwestern cities overtook it in importance by the turn of the twentieth century, Cincinnati still grew, making public markets like Findlay all the more important.

Like in other cities, Cincinnati's local government built, maintained and regulated market spaces. Establishing itself early on as a steward for the food supply, the City of Cincinnati coordinated and regulated the practices of wholesalers (also known as commission merchants) and retailers. As the landlord of public markets, the city earned revenue from them, and in the early and mid-nineteenth century, this financial aspect often operated as a key motive for city involvement. By the early 1900s, Cincinnati and other urban governments were taking cues from federal leadership and becoming more proactive in regulating markets and other public space for the public's good. As the United States underwent numerous reforms around 1900 to make America safer, cleaner and more equitable, cities enacted public health reforms to make markets and food safer. Throughout the 1800s and early 1900s, municipal officials and administrators—even though corrupt at times—cared about their cities, taking deep pride in dense urban cores with thriving businesses.

Tandem with Cincinnati's commercial and industrial growth were the immigrants and migrants coming there. Throughout the 1800s and early 1900s, the city attracted people from Great Britain, newcomers from various German-speaking states in central Europe and Yiddish-speaking Jewish immigrants from Russia and eastern Europe, in addition to other groups like Italians and Hungarians. Earlier waves of immigrants—most of them Germans—were more affluent, in part because of industrialization in their homelands. Their skill and wealth enabled them to build Findlay's market square and other downtown real estate. But later generations of immigrants from eastern Europe—who were poorer because of the conditions there—also ran businesses at Findlay and lived above the shops, creating a dense arrangement of multi-unit housing along the market square. The different peoples coming into Over-the-Rhine mirrored waves of immigration in other cities throughout the 1800s and early 1900s and how those immigrants made

U.S. cities by creating dense, diverse neighborhoods—a vital cycle disrupted when the United States closed its borders to immigrants from the 1920s to the 1960s. Thereafter, second- and third-generation immigrants continued to run Findlay Market, and shoppers were quick to remind anyone that Findlay's ethnic heritage was a key reason why they continued to shop there.

In these midcentury years, Appalachians and then African American families moved into the neighborhood, forming the next waves of shoppers to patronize the market and furthering Findlay Market's important cultural diversity. But African Americans—who became the majority of the population around Findlay Market and in Over-the-Rhine by the 1990s—remained excluded from business and real estate opportunities at and near the market. Stories of people of color there shine a light on cities' role in racial discrimination, particularly how urban America came to be "a black ghetto." In Cincinnati, from the early 1800s onward, African Americans were forced to live in certain sections of basin neighborhoods—first the riverfront, then the West End and later displaced to Over-the-Rhine—confined to the worst housing in these neighborhoods. Many suburbs, which had emerged as early as the mid-1800s, rejected African American residents. When Black families moved into the area around Findlay Market, generations of discrimination worked against their social mobility. Denied home and business loans, they were limited to few employment opportunities. Physically and financially segregated, African Americans became very poor in the hearts of U.S. cities by the late 1900s. In 1990—when Over-the-Rhine was 70 percent Black—60 percent of all occupied units in Over-the-Rhine were government-subsidized low-income ones.

When, beginning in the late 1800s, the immigrant families who built and lived around Findlay Market moved to hilltop and farther-out suburbs, they initiated the long historical process of urban decentralization. Around 1900, city leaders thought that this growing separation between suburban residences and downtown commerce and industry was good, although poorer families remained living in increasingly deteriorated housing in the city center. By the 1920s, Cincinnati leadership mirrored other city governments in further embracing this sprawl. City officials remade their downtowns—through demolition of buildings and streets—into anti-dense, modern spaces for new offices, transportation access and automobile parking, the idea being that people would drive to and work in the city center but not live there. Consequentially, Cincinnati demolished its downtown public markets over the mid-twentieth century, making room for highways and parking lots. Findlay Market was left alone only because it was not in the way of proposed highways or other new construction. Across the United States, many other cities demolished their downtown retail and wholesale food markets too, making way for new development. That people, as they moved from the urban core, shopped at chain stores near their homes further justified the demolition of urban markets.

In the post–World War II era, the federal government subsidized suburban sprawl for white families, hastening urban decentralization and downtown demolition. With the residential exodus out of city centers, business and industry followed shoppers and pursued lower tax rates in suburban, rural and other remote locations, leaving city tax revenue and resources severely depleted. While municipal leaders thought that they were doing their cities a service by making them more "modern" through anti-density, much of the twentieth century was instead a low point for urban planning, when city officials failed to be stewards for the oldest sections of the city. From 1950 to 2000, Cincinnati lost 35 percent of its population. In these decades, Findlay Market managed to maintain a steady customer base of both suburban and more local shoppers. But it nonetheless reflected the troubled times. In 2000, one-fourth of its storefronts were vacant, and only eight people—across thirty-three large multi-unit buildings—lived above the market square.

By the turn of the twenty-first century, the city of Cincinnati reinvented—and in many ways renewed—its relationship with its urban core, as Findlay Market again shows us. Beginning in the 1960s, with federal aid, leadership in U.S. cities slowly realized that widespread divestment of downtown neighborhoods was a social injustice and public health crisis since poor minorities lived there. City officials also acknowledged that the larger metropolitan area existed only because of the city center. If the center was sick, something was off with the entire city. Embracing historic preservation for the first time, municipal leaders in Cincinnati and other cities gradually realized that historic fabric mattered to people and that it could re-attract businesses and residents to the core. With this mindset and goal, the City of Cincinnati renovated Findlay Market's markethouse in the 1970s using federal aid and in the 1980s got Over-the-Rhine designated a national historic district. Around 2000, the city—partnering with private development—renovated the markethouse again, as well as the market square and the area around it, hoping to get businesses (and eventually residents) to fill up the vacant storefronts and thousands of empty apartment units in Over-the-Rhine. Since then, the city has continued to work with private developers and the new Corporation for Findlay Market, the market's nonprofit manager, to renovate and fill up the market square.

This real estate revival clues us in to the urban revitalization occurring across many U.S. cities right now, with people returning to live and work in city centers again—a positive development but not one without challenges. With the stated mission of redeveloping Over-the-Rhine into a mixed-income neighborhood, the City of Cincinnati has actively worked to mitigate displacement of existing residents by incentivizing low-income housing, but its efforts have not satisfied everyone in Cincinnati. Over-the-Rhine has become a contested space like many other urban-core neighborhoods seeing reinvestment, where people and their local governments are trying to figure out—perhaps for the first time—how to have a truly mixed-income, class- and race-diverse city center.

In spite of major obstacles like white flight and suburban sprawl, a key reason why Findlay Market survived is that it always had shoppers who loved it. (Of course, this was true for many other markets that got demolished, and in this way, Findlay was just luckier to be tucked away from highway paths.) Still, at all times of its history, including up through the late twentieth century when so many people had abandoned downtown, shoppers maintained a deep loyalty to the place. What were people's reasons for loving Findlay? They commented that it had an "old-timey" feel. They liked that it was run by immigrants with a variety of unique products. They appreciated that you could hear vendors speaking different languages as you shopped. They especially liked that you could form lasting relationships with merchants. They also shopped there because much of it was competitively affordable.

In these reasons, we see what's great about cities around the world—density, diversity of people, great architecture, opportunities for business and more. People could articulate that they loved these aspects of Findlay, but many could not apply the same logic to the rest of Cincinnati's old inner city, to care about it in the same way as the market. That kind of attitude was a major reason why the area around the market suffered so much throughout the twentieth century.

Now, we are seeing more and more people come back to cities. That gives us an opportunity to appreciate how the oldest parts of our cities—both the people and the built environment there—matter deeply to the rest of the metropolitan whole. This book—on the surface, about a beloved market—gets at this larger point: that we cannot understand the significance of Findlay Market without also acknowledging the entire city center and its history.

CHAPTER 1

ONE OF MANY MARKETS

THE FIRST DECADES OF FINDLAY MARKET

F ounded in 1788 on the Ohio River, Cincinnati grew dramatically in the early 1800s to become the largest city west of the Appalachian Mountains. As a riverboat port, Cincinnati was a crucial part of interstate commerce. Constructed from 1825 to 1845, the Miami and Erie Canal—which stretched down from Lake Erie in the north—wound its way through Cincinnati's downtown basin, further making the city a commercial hub. Cincinnati quickly became a major exporter of pork, whiskey and beer, and this explosion of trade and business attracted many to the city. People settled within the city's small valley, north of the river and south of the surrounding hills. These factors—growing commerce and immigration and a physically confined urban core—resulted in the city becoming, for a time, one of the most densely populated in the country. Urban public markets quickly developed, feeding the growing downtown population and contributing to the city's commercial success.

Cincinnati's first white settlers were affluent people of English, Scottish and Welsh backgrounds, as well as poorer Irish immigrants. They lived along the riverfront and slowly spread north along the city's early grid street pattern. African Americans were other early residents, residing in segregated areas along the river and in the basin. About one mile north of the water sat dense forest, slowly being cleared for farming and then urban development. In the 1830s and 1840s, German-speaking immigrants arrived in Cincinnati in significant numbers as a part of a larger immigration trend that saw more than 1.5 million Germans coming to America by 1860. Within U.S.

Top: Cincinnati in 1800. *Courtesy of the Public Library of Cincinnati and Hamilton County.*

Bottom: Cincinnati in 1830—a growing city, with development concentrated in the basin. *Courtesy of the Public Library of Cincinnati and Hamilton County.*

cities, Germans were like other immigrants in that they settled in ethnic enclaves. In downtown Cincinnati, Germans chose the area far north of the riverfront—a section of land bounded by the Miami and Erie Canal on the south and west, Sycamore Street on the east and the hills to the north. So many Germans moved there that the canal was nicknamed the Rhine River, thus earning the area the name "Over-the-Rhine." The northern half of Over-the-Rhine, past Liberty Street, was called the Northern Liberties since it was outside the corporation limits until 1849. By 1840, the Northern Liberties already had a German population of 8,000.[2]

In 1855, the City of Cincinnati established a market within these Northern Liberties. Land for the market came from James Findlay, an early developer of Over-the-Rhine. Findlay, born in 1770 in Pennsylvania, moved to Cincinnati with his wife, Jane, in 1793 and thereafter became a mover and a shaker in local and state politics. He served as Cincinnati's mayor twice,

Cincinnati in 1855. The map shows Findlay Market between "North" and "Findley" Streets. *Courtesy of the Public Library of Cincinnati and Hamilton County.*

fought in the War of 1812 and later was an Ohio congressman from 1825 to 1833. As an early speculator and investor in Cincinnati, he and a business partner—lawyer Jeptha Garrard—bought a significant amount of land in the Northern Liberties and recorded a town plat in 1833, officially establishing the area as "Findlay's Woods." With this plat, Findlay also established an open area for a public farmers' market and a general store because there was no such thing that far north. Findlay died in 1835 and Garrard in 1837 before they could build the market. Findlay's widow inherited the land, but it was not until after her death in 1851 that construction of Findlay Market began. Executors of Findlay's estate gave the land to the city, and German immigrant Nikolaus Hoeffer served as the property agent and administrator for it along with Findlay's other holdings.[3]

Findlay Market was built along Elder Street, bounded to the west by Elm Street and the east by Race Street. In 1852, Hoeffer laid the cornerstone for

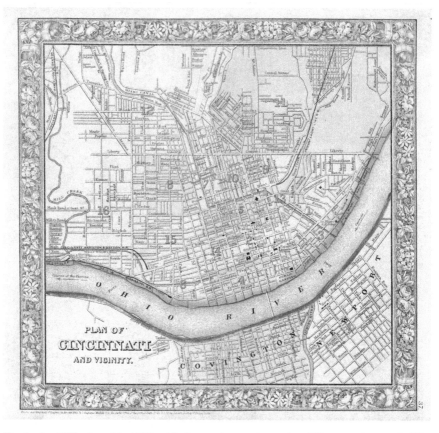

The basin of Cincinnati in 1864, with the numbers representing different voting wards. The canal cut through downtown and defined Over-the-Rhine to the north (wards 7, 9, 10 and some of 11), the central business district to the south (wards 1 through 5, 13 and 14) and the West End to the west (wards 6, 8, 12, 15 and 16). *Courtesy of Wikipedia.*

the market, including with it several bottles of wine from his own collection. Three years later, an open-sided markethouse with a cast- and wrought-iron frame opened for business. Interior butcher stalls accompanied exterior removable produce stands. Rimming the markethouse on Elder Street, rowhouses were erected, each with a storefront, creating a commercial square around Findlay Market.[4]

From its first decades of operation, Findlay Market tells us much about urban America in the mid- to late 1800s. That Cincinnati grew tremendously over the nineteenth century, requiring the development of fresh urban markets to support its population, underscored the urbanization occurring throughout the United States in these years. The City of Cincinnati established downtown markets for meat, produce, dry goods and other items, showing us how municipal governments throughout the nation were involved in their cities' early growth. They intervened in their local economies to make sure business thrived and to guarantee that municipal reserves received funds—but also to make sure that residents had access to quality food and goods. In Over-the-Rhine, Germans built and maintained Findlay Market's stands, stalls and storefronts, reminding us of the important role that immigrants played in the early urban and commercial development in the country. Finally, business proprietors, their families and other immigrants lived above Findlay Market's storefronts. Their lives and stories reveal hardships of nineteenth-century living and how much of it fell on women.

URBAN MARKETS IN CINCINNATI AND NINETEENTH-CENTURY AMERICA

Indicative of a healthy and growing city, Findlay Market joined other downtown markets that emerged as the city developed northward. Emulating European cities, American municipalities—including Cincinnati—created, managed and regulated urban wholesale and retail markets as their populations grew. City governments saw them as a key financial venture and a public health service.

In developing its food infrastructure downtown, Cincinnati located its wholesale markets close to the river for water (and later rail) transportation access. Retail markets—which also housed some wholesalers—were located throughout the downtown basin, following residential development there. Many sat along or near the Miami and Erie Canal. This was common across U.S. cities where municipal governments sited markets near water or other points of transportation access.

In 1801, Cincinnati's first public market was established in a rudimentary wooden markethouse on the riverfront where farmers on boat, horse and wagon brought their goods to sell—everything from chicken to fish, eggs, beef, corn, whiskey, venison and rare delicacies like bear and soft-shelled turtle. In 1804, the market moved north a few blocks to east–west running Pearl Street located between Sycamore and Main Streets, and in 1816, it moved east to Broadway and Sycamore Streets and was then known as the Lower Market. West of it, on Pearl Street between Elm and Central Avenue, was the Pearl Street Market. The city built another market at Fifth and Main Streets that was later moved one block west to Walnut and Vine Streets. In

Findlay Market, circa 1921, its iron frame partially visible. *Courtesy of Don Prout, Cincinnati Views.*

1826, the Sixth Street Market began, located on Sixth Street between Plum and Western Row (now Central Avenue). Three years later, in 1829, Wade Street Market went up, made from reclaimed wood taken from the earliest church in Cincinnati, First Presbyterian. That same year, in 1829, the Miami and Erie Canal Market was established on Court Street between Vine and Walnut. Many others followed: by the start of the Civil War in 1861, there were already nine. In 1864, the city demolished Canal Market and built the Court Street Market there.[5]

Most of Cincinnati's early markets operated similarly. Each had a central markethouse with interior stalls (usually for butchers) and exterior stands (usually for produce) surrounded by a square of dense buildings; each building had a commercial storefront. This created a permanent market square. Early colonial-era markets lacked buildings—they were just street markets—but in the early 1800s, cities decided to build structures to offer businesses a more permanent space. Cities located early markethouses in the middle of wide squares or streets—on public property—to avoid having to buy buildings on a city block.[6]

Long and narrow in design, early markethouses like Findlay's were shaped so that traffic could move around them and wagons and carts could pull up along the sides. Most early nineteenth-century markethouses were simple wood-frame buildings with pitched roofs supported by load-bearing walls or a post-and-beam system. Cincinnati's Fifth Street Market resembled such

Sixth Street Market in the early 1900s. Built by famous architect Samuel Hannaford and his company, Samuel Hannaford and Sons, the Sixth Street Market signaled a new era of more permanent markethouses, designed to last. *Courtesy of the Public Library of Cincinnati and Hamilton County.*

construction with its three-hundred-foot-long wooden house. While citizens relied on public markets as their primary food source, early Americans were less attached to the physical space than we are today, especially since most were wood houses designed to fail eventually. People expected that their markets would be occasionally torn down but would be soon replaced by a new one. Later, cities built markethouses with metal and stone frames, used brick and glass for infill and added decorative features like cupolas, making the markethouses durable. Findlay's cast- and iron-wrought frame was a part of this trend. Similarly, the Sixth Street Market's butcher house, built in 1895, originally resembled a simple shed but was later added onto with masonry materials, resulting in an impressive façade. Also indicative of its permanence, it had a stone foundation like other downtown markets.[7]

Cities located early public markets—like this one in Cincinnati—on extra-wide streets to create market squares. *Courtesy of the Public Library of Cincinnati and Hamilton County.*

Inside markethouses, initially only meat was sold, as was the case at Findlay for many years. Meat was the most profitable trade, making butchers able to pay the higher rents for inside stalls. Inside Findlay, resembling other markethouses, glass display cases lined the long central aisle, featuring fresh cuts of meat. Meat was also hung on wall hooks within the stalls, and sawdust covered the floor to absorb dripping blood. Lacking refrigeration, merchants used ice during the day to chill perishables. At the end of each business day, they removed meat and other items to store them off-site.[8]

Surrounding the markethouses, street vendors erected stands—taken down on off-market days—where customers could buy fresh fruits and vegetables, flowers, live poultry and rabbits. On market days, vendors brought their goods into the market square on horse-drawn wagons, hauling their supply from home or warehouses. Under canvas-covered stands, food and other items were displayed in open bowls, barrels and baskets. Wagons and milling shoppers competed for space with the stands, making the area outside the markethouse bustling. Working out of small stands, street vendors were unable to sell as much—and thus make as much—as inside butchers and merchants in nearby brick-and-mortar storefronts.

Echoing the other market squares in downtown Cincinnati, Findlay Market's main house was surrounded by buildings along Elder Street. Erected in the late 1850s, 1860s and 1870s, two-, three- and four-story structures framed in the markethouse to its north and south on Elder. Longer front to back than they were side to side, they were made from wood and brick construction. Commercial storefronts on the first floors

Pearl Street Market in the early 1900s. *Courtesy of the Public Library of Cincinnati and Hamilton County.*

had large display windows within cast-iron columns. Awnings shaded the sidewalks in front, enabling vendors to shade and protect their wares. Above storefronts were residential quarters where storefront proprietors lived with their families. Below, stone foundation basements offered cool storage. Most buildings on the square were made of soft, porous brick. Already then, as early as the 1860s, wood-frame structures were becoming less common in Over-the-Rhine since, like with markethouses, people wanted to use more durable materials in building construction. The occasional breezeway—a passageway from the front of a building along its side to its rear—broke up the dense frontage of these buildings along Elder Street. In the rear or along the sides of these buildings, residents found small wood-frame sheds, privies and exterior stairs to reach upper-level apartments. These architectural patterns that defined the area immediately around the markethouse also characterized the rest of the Over-the-Rhine.

SANBORN MAP

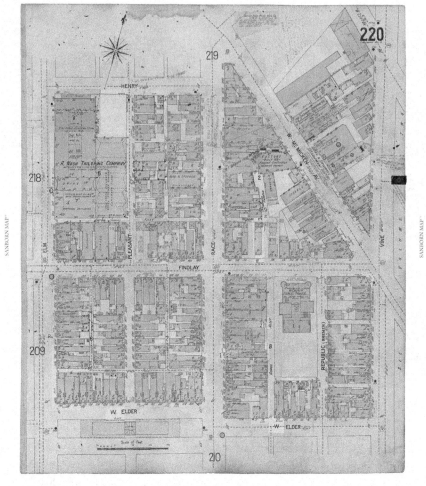

SANBORN MAP

This page and opposite: Sanborn Fire Insurance maps of the Findlay Market area, 1904. The maps show Findlay Market to the north and south of Elder Street. Notice how dense the area surrounding the market was, populated by narrow two-, three- and four-story buildings. Over-the-Rhine's buildings were Italianate in design and "shotgun style" (long and narrow) in shape. Residents who lived above storefronts typically used a breezeway—a long, narrow passage along the side of the building—to access a side or rear stair system to take them upstairs. Wood-frame buildings initially composed most of the housing in Over-the-Rhine, followed by brick masonry ones built in the late 1800s. Privies and sheds existed behind buildings and in courtyards, as the smaller shapes on the Sanborn maps show. *Courtesy of the Public Library of Cincinnati and Hamilton County.*

In these storefronts opposite the Findlay markethouse, early shops sold produce, dry and baked goods, clothing, shoes and boots, furniture, hardware, notions and chinaware. There were several early coffeehouses, a blacksmith and even an umbrella shop. In the large four-story building to the immediate northeast of the market, an apothecary offered customers tonics and drugs. Inside these different storefronts, customers usually found wood counters toward the front, behind which were shelves of packaged goods. Many shops had glass display cases showing items like candy or cigarettes. In dry goods and grocery stores, bushel baskets and wood crates toward the rear of the storefront offered bulk items next to a scale.[9]

In its role as landlord, the City of Cincinnati set the days and times that markets could operate. This was essential in early American cities since farmers, moving produce and animals into cities, needed a set time to sell their goods. Like other cities, Cincinnati made sure that market retailers and wholesalers adhered to market times, only sold their goods then and there and did not hoard or spread false rumors to create an incorrect impression about available supply. The city maintained a Bureau of Markets, Weights and Measures, with a market superintendent who weighed and inspected goods, sending damaged ones to local prisoners. Above all else, the superintendent's job was to ensure the quality of market goods in an era long before federal consumer protection legislation. Certain "unclean" animal meats like dog and cat were not allowed to be sold. You could not slaughter a horse within the market square. You could not smoke tobacco, be intoxicated or idle in the market. At the end of each market day, the superintendent required that each stand and stall "be thoroughly cleaned, and all animal and vegetable rubbish to be removed from the marketplace, and each butcher shall cause his tables, meatblocks and other fixtures to be thoroughly scraped and cleaned." Cincinnati's city council also established a Committee on Markets that regularly met with the local Board of Health to monitor sanitation at the markets.[10]

Outside of the markethouses, cities further regulated the food trade by dictating rates, loads and hours of operation for carriers and suppliers. In Cincinnati, the city monitored goods coming from steamboats along the Ohio River, from boats along the Miami and Erie Canal and later from riverfront railroad depots. Goods were usually placed in nearby wholesale warehouses and later moved to various urban retail markets like Findlay. Across urban America, the building and maintenance of urban markets reflected highly involved city government that saw itself as a steward of the urban food supply.

Of course, city business interests were also important, sometimes to the detriment of public markets. In 1863, the City of Cincinnati decided to lease its market on Pearl Street between Elm and Central Avenues to the Cincinnati and Indiana Railroad Company, which wanted to use the markethouse as a passenger depot. The sale "will transform it into a source of revenue," city council decided, "as well as tend to remove from our midst what has been considered ever since its construction, a cesspool for generating sickness and disease." The city did not take responsibility for the lack of hygiene at the market, and it viewed the transaction only in how the railroad would bring in more commerce and increase the value of downtown property. Across

U.S. cities in the early and mid-1800s, local governments had a tendency to siphon revenue from markets into other city coffers, causing market buildings to deteriorate. All the while, cities still charged vendors rent and, for the best stalls inside markethouses, extra premiums. It would only be at the turn of the twentieth century—during an era of city reform—that municipal governments expended more city money on their markets to better ensure their safety and durability.[11]

Seeing as it was impossible to monitor all market activity, city regulation was uneven and often ineffective. In Cincinnati, there were butchers, for instance, who rented a market stall from the city but then, in an effort to make a side profit, subleased the space to "bushwackers"—amateur butchers known to handle inferior meat and undercut the prices of nearby quality butchers. It fell to customers—primarily women doing the shopping—to negotiate a flawed system. Women often haggled, realizing their consumer power as they dealt with imperfect quality and dishonest merchants.[12]

City regulation of markets grew over the 1800s as industrialization changed American patterns of production and consumption. Early urban markets in the United States functioned through a close relationship between farmer and customer. Shoppers frequented different retail urban markets, getting their groceries and supplies from merchants who bought directly from farmers. While early Cincinnati imported certain items from outside the region—things like coffee, tea, sugar and molasses—many grains (corn, wheat, flour, oats, barley, rye) as well as produce, dry goods and animal meat were local. From regional farms, goods reached Cincinnati's urban markets by traveling along the Ohio River or along the Miami and Erie Canal. Using wagons, farmers also drove goods into cities using a network of turnpikes, with many linking up with the canal. Farmers also walked livestock—local cattle, sheep and hogs—on foot from Ohio and Indiana farms to the city. There, animals went to slaughterhouses for butchering and packing. Commission merchants—strategically located along the canal and riverfront—bought the meat and sold it to butchers at Findlay.

Beginning around the time of Findlay Market's founding, these relationships and processes began to change. With industrialization and a revolution in transportation brought on by railroads, foods and goods came from and were exported outside local channels. Beginning in the 1840s and 1850s, Cincinnati had access to several regional railroad lines, up to seven by World War I. The western edge of the downtown riverfront, near many markets, was a key exchange and terminus area for many of these railroads.[13]

The Miami and Erie Canal at Findlay Street, just to the west of the market. The canal was an important conduit for getting food and goods into the city. *Courtesy of the Public Library of Cincinnati and Hamilton County.*

Railroads suddenly enabled Cincinnati and other cities to import and export goods from far away. This was good news for farmers and other producers who could participate in growing markets and were freed from earlier climate constraints. For instance, with refrigerated railcars, already-slaughtered livestock could travel long distances without spoilage, regardless of the time of year. But with these changes, producers like farmers paid dearly to transport and store their goods in cities since they had to compensate a growing number of middlemen along the way. This included buying agents who purchased goods directly from farmers and then moved the goods to cities. Once in cities, goods collected in wholesale warehouses and storage facilities where retail merchants, like those at Findlay Market, purchased supplies either from commission merchants or from jobbers who bought from wholesalers and then resold to retailers. With railroads and associated transportation changes, customers had access to a greater variety of foods and goods, but they increasingly came from outside the area, from California and southern states. Furthermore, the growing number of middlemen added to production and distribution costs, which were usually passed on to the customer. Around 1900, a family expected to spend up to half of their monthly expenditures on food, with meat being the most expensive item to purchase. All of these changes meant that production and distribution of goods were spatially separated in unprecedented ways. While not always successful, city regulation of urban markets increasingly had to make sure that food and goods retained high quality as they endured longer travel times.[14]

THOSE WHO BUILT THE MARKET: OVER-THE-RHINE'S EARLY IMMIGRANTS

The initial families who ran businesses and lived at Findlay Market were immigrants, overwhelmingly German-speaking ones, and many of them fairly well off, giving them the ability to start long-lasting commercial ventures at the market. Throughout the mid-1800s, they helped to transform Over-the-Rhine into a dense ethnic enclave. They imported their language, politics and cultural beliefs into the neighborhood, but they also acted on American issues like slavery, becoming U.S. citizens in their own way. From its beginning, Findlay Market, like other public markets in U.S. cities, served as a vital hub for that immigrant culture and those immigrant-run businesses.

A diversity of Germans—Catholics, Protestants and Jews; liberals and conservatives; speakers of different dialects—immigrated to the United States. Germany was not a nation until 1871, so prior to that, Germans came from different German states and principalities—especially from Bavaria, Baden and Württemberg—as well as the Austro-Hungarian empire, Switzerland and elsewhere in Europe. Nikolaus Hoeffer—the German immigrant who laid Findlay Market's cornerstone—came from the farming village of Rülzheim in the Palatinate region, then under Bavarian control. His family—like most Germans and most immigrants to the United States—left for economic reasons, with poverty driving them to leave. The Hoeffers had a subsistence farm and eked out a living as small linen weavers, neither of which kept them afloat. From around 1750 to 1850, the German population across central Europe doubled, and with that population pressure, many agrarian workers struggled to own their own or enough land to make a living. For skilled artisans and the growing urban working class, uneven industrialization and lack of access to social mobility pushed many to emigrate for better work conditions and opportunities elsewhere. The Hoeffers left in 1832, going to New York City and then Cincinnati.[15]

Germans came to the United States in record numbers. Between the 1830s and 1880s, Germans were never less than one-fourth of all immigrants. While most settled outside cities, the rest chose large cities like New York City and cities throughout the Midwest with growing German populations—like Cincinnati. By 1850, 60 percent of Over-the-Rhine's population was German. Since economic pressures pushed out many Germans, a good portion arrived in U.S. cities as trained artisans in brewing, baking, butchering, distilling, cabinetry, cigar-making and machinery. With such skills, early German immigrants tended to be a more affluent group than those of other ethnicities who came from more impoverished or oppressive homelands. In Over-the-Rhine, many of the neighborhood's first German families owned their own businesses, built housing stock throughout the neighborhood and founded many of the city's important financial and cultural institutions—like Findlay Market.[16]

After immigrating, Hoeffer—with his agricultural skills—leased land on Findlay's estate, a few blocks north of where Findlay Market would be. There, at the corner of Elm Street and McMicken Avenue, he tended his crop until, in 1850, he chose to go into real estate development and property management. After Findlay's widow died in 1851, Hoeffer became the property agent and administrator for Findlay's holdings, helping the city to construct Findlay Market. Afterward, Hoeffer maintained his real estate office to the immediate east of the market.[17]

Like Hoeffer's real estate business, examples of early and longstanding German businesses at Findlay Market abound—especially within the markethouse, where stalls tended to stay within families over generations. The Spies' deli was one such spot, selling cheese, sausages, sauerkraut and pickles from the late 1800s through the 1970s. Stephen Spies—an immigrant from Prussia, born in 1854—immigrated to the United States and established a shop at Sixth and Main Streets in 1879. From there, he established a stall in Findlay Market's markethouse as well as another deli north of the market on McMicken Avenue. His sons—including William Wilson—helped him run the business.[18]

Outside the markethouse, early German families started produce stands that also lasted for years. Theodor Kunkel began a pickle and sauerkraut stand there in 1855 after emigrating from Neuhütten, Bavaria. He also operated one at Court Street Market, as was common among early vendors—the two markets being open on different days. After he

William Wilson Spies (1899–1973) later in life with his son, Wilson Spies Jr. (1926–2013), as they walked at Findlay Market. After Stephen Spies (1854–1913) started the family cheese store, his son William Wilson took over. Wilson Jr. then carried on the tradition at Findlay Market, even starting his own stand. Wilson Jr.'s eldest son, Willie, then continued the business. Willie married Debbie Nalsh of Nalsh Bakery, whose family was as deeply rooted in Findlay Market as the Spieses were. *Courtesy of Karen Baum.*

died in 1886, his children and other descendants continued the operation for the next 150 years or so.[19]

Within the storefronts rimming the market square, early German merchants were similarly well positioned to start long-lasting businesses.

Federal censuses reveal a considerable amount of personal and real estate wealth among these families—several hundred thousand dollars and sometimes more in personal and real estate assets by the 1870s and 1880s. Some used a humble Findlay Market storefront to launch what became a major business later. William H. Alms ran a dry goods shop at 112 West Elder on the north side of the markethouse from 1859 to 1861. Alms—a second-generation German immigrant born in Cincinnati in 1842—then teamed up with his elder brother Frederick and a cousin, William Doepke, in 1865 to form the Alms & Doepke Company, which became the leading wholesale and retail dry goods company in the city and eventually the largest in Ohio.[20]

Christian Weber—a shoe and boot store owner at Findlay Market and friend of the Alms family—was another early merchant who grew a significant amount of wealth from his business. Upon his death in 1877 (when he was thrown from a horse buggy), he had millions of dollars in personal and real estate, including farmland on the west side of Cincinnati in Green Township, where his sister and her family lived. Born in 1831 in Koenigsbach, Bavaria, Weber was married to Rosina (née Beiswanger), a German woman from Stuttgart, with whom he had eleven children. The family lived above the shoe business at Findlay, and after Christian's death, Rosina ran the business through the 1880s. Belying the family's wealth, the Webers moved between three different storefronts at the market square throughout the 1860s before settling at 128 West Elder on the north side. This storefront hopping within the buildings surrounding the market was fairly common at the market, and to accommodate it, nonstructural demising interior walls within storefronts were often moved around or removed. "Store, with or without rooms," read one advertisement for a storefront just east of the market.[21]

In transforming Over-the-Rhine into an immigrant enclave, Germans like the Webers established a number of social institutions to help other Germans. Well-off merchants at the market used their accumulating wealth to support benevolent and mutual aid societies for other Germans as they aged, experienced poverty or illness or left widows or orphans. Several of these groups met regularly at Findlay Market, indicative that it was a central point in their community. These kinds of organizations were common across different immigrant groups in U.S. cities where community leaders set up rudimentary welfare systems, and members paid dues and could borrow money when needed.

The sons of German immigrants, brothers John and Henry Kruse ran a successful dry goods shop on the south side of Findlay's square from the

Christian (1831–1877) and Rosa Weber (1839–1902). Christian was a business entrepreneur, landowner in the Cincinnati area and a gifted bass violinist who pushed his children to pursue music too. Like other early Findlay Market families, the Webers became a prominent German family in Over-the-Rhine. *Courtesy of Vickie Hahn.*

1860s until 1895. When John died in 1908, he had around $1 million in assets, some of which his will delved out to local German charities. He gave more than $100,000 to the German General Protestant Orphan Society; the *Deutsches Altenheim*, a nursing home for elderly German immigrant men; the German Protestant Widow's Home; and to St. Paulus Kirche, a church three blocks south of Findlay Market. His generosity not only underscored how well his dry goods shop had performed but also signaled his strong immigrant and ethnic culture.[22]

Wealth—and a strong sense of immigrant community—also propelled Germans at Findlay Market to create mutual savings societies, credit unions, banks and building and loan associations that allowed members a chance at home and business ownership. Prior to the 1930s, mortgages required a massive down payment (up to 50 percent) and had to be paid back within only a few years, making homeownership elusive for most Americans. Building and loan associations circumvented this problem by enabling members, who held shares in that association, to borrow on interest for a mortgage. Organized in 1885, the Findlay Market Loan and Building Company was one such lender, operating from 107 West Elder's storefront on Findlay Market's square in the late nineteenth century.

This page and opposite, top: Two of Christian and Rosa's sons, Adam (1854–1890) and John C. Weber (1855–1938), became famous musicians, following Christian's musical inclinations. Adam directed the orchestra at Heuck's Opera House on Vine Street in Over-the-Rhine, as well as the band at Wielert's Café, another famous spot in Over-the-Rhine. He died young, in his early thirties, of tuberculosis. His younger brother John was the director of the famous Prize Band of America. Among other accomplishments, he wrote a piece for and conducted at the 1904 World's Fair in St. Louis. *Courtesy of Vickie Hahn and the Library of Congress.*

WEBERS PRIZE BAND, AT THE OAKS AUDITORIUM, PORTLAND, OREGON.
E.SOWELL, Foto.

Right: Aside from Adam and John Weber, their younger sister Carrie (1874–1953) was also a musician: she graduated from Cincinnati College of Music and wrote music for her brother John's band. She married David Schorr, a prominent attorney, who helped to found one of the political parties in Cincinnati, the reformist Charter Committee. *Courtesy of Vickie Hahn.*

The will of John Kruse (circa 1825–1908). He never married, so in his will, he bequeathed money to various charitable societies, many of them for German immigrants. He and his younger brother Henry (1833–1924) ran a dry goods shop at Findlay Market at 101 West Elder (at the corner of Race and Elder Streets) from the 1860s until 1895. The building stayed in the family until the 1950s. John and Henry were from Hanover, born to Bernard (1794–1881) and Margaret (Bosche) (1798–1871). The family immigrated to Cincinnati in the 1840s and lived above their Findlay Market storefront for many years. *Courtesy of Ancestry.com.*

Charles Kuchenbuch—a longstanding and influential German baker at Findlay Market—founded it and served as its president when he ran his bakery out of 106 West Elder's storefront.[23]

Kuchenbuch's business lasted at Findlay Market from 1869 until the early 1900s. Born in 1843 in the city of Werkhausen in what is now western Germany, Kuchenbuch immigrated to Cincinnati in the early 1850s with his family. Along with other nearby German merchants, he was a member of the *Deutsche Pionierverein*, the largest German organization in Cincinnati. Members had to be male immigrants over forty years old and residents of Cincinnati for at least twenty-five years. Founded in 1868, its goal was to create a community for Germans and German Americans and to preserve the history of that community, which it did in part through its nationally recognized journal, *Der Deutsche Pionier*. Nikolaus Hoeffer was a founding member of this group. While the *Pionierverein* was considered one of the most influential groups, Germans maintained numerous cultural organizations in Over-the-Rhine. Many of them met at Findlay Market, making it a hub for their ethnic pride.[24]

While they invested in cultural preservation, German immigrants also engaged in U.S. politics, importing their beliefs and applying them here. Coming from repressive states in Europe, many Germans immigrated with liberal values. Believing in representative government, they opposed slavery on arrival. Many, then, helped form the Republican Party in the 1850s because it (generally speaking) stood for free waged labor, not slavery and its expansion. Many of these Germans also fought in the Civil War for the Union army. Numerous merchants at Findlay Market took up arms in this capacity, including Christian Weber and Henry Kruse. "Forty-Eighters"—the politically liberal refugees who fled Europe around 1848—were passionate supporters of the Union. In 1848, spurred by another French revolution, farmers, peasants, artisans, industrial workers and intellectuals in central and western European states demanded powerful political and socioeconomic reforms. People organized against unrepresentative and repressive government, unfair work conditions and the growing gap between rich and poor, creating a wave of revolutionary activity. Regimes in power won, though, resulting in the exodus of Forty-Eighters from Europe. Many German Forty-Eighters came to Cincinnati, settling in Over-the-Rhine with their liberal, antislavery values.[25]

But the other Civil War–era party, the Democrat Party, had German followers, too, reminding us that one word to describe an entire immigrant group—such as *Germans*—does not capture how complex its makeup was. At the time of the Civil War, Democrats differentiated themselves from Republicans by their support of states' rights and their dislike of a large federal government. German Democrats tended to be immigrants who came to the United States early in the 1800s—prior to the 1848 revolutions—and who had done well for themselves; many had conservative religious or political leanings. Hoeffer was a longtime Democrat. He served as the city commissioner as a Democrat from 1863 to 1866 and later as the local Democrat party chairman. Upon Hoeffer's death, the *Cincinnati Enquirer* noted in his obituary that Hoeffer was once "mobbed" at his home by Findlay Market for his "avowed States Rights principles." Nicholas Diehl—a longstanding produce merchant at Findlay Market and a rare wholesaler one—was another German Democrat, serving as an Ohio state representative after he retired from his commission produce business. At Findlay Market, he worked out of his building at 108

Nicholas Diehl (1849–1932). Nicholas was the son of George Diehl, a farmer from Frankfurt, and Anna Marie (Becker). He had several older siblings, some born in Germany and some in Ohio like him. Growing up in Cincinnati, Nicholas attended St. John's Parochial Schools and then learned the trade of machine moulding before he became a commission merchant. He married twice—first in 1873 to Josephine (Butscha) (1852–1897) and then after her death to Josephine (Ervent) (1874–1952) in 1897. The latter had seven children, six of whom lived past infancy. As a fruit and vegetable merchant for many years at Findlay Markey, Nicholas was the treasurer for the Findlay Market Loan and Building Company and was an active member of the Democrat Party in Cincinnati, serving as a delegate to many Democratic conventions. *Courtesy of the Public Library of Cincinnati and Hamilton County.*

West Elder on the market's north side from 1870 through the early 1900s. He lived upstairs with his extended family.[26]

In early Findlay Market, German merchants not only retained stalls and stores for many years, but for those who owned one of the buildings along the square, they also held that property for generations. The large four-story brick structure to the immediate northeast of Findlay Market housed the Muhlberg family's pharmacy from 1867 to the early 1960s, making it one of the longest-running businesses at Findlay Market and one of the longest-running drugstores in the city. The building, built in 1857 by German druggist Adolph Stierle, housed Stierle's apothecary business until William Muhlberg bought it in 1867. Born in 1823 in Eisenberg, Saxony, Muhlberg studied medicine and pharmacy at the University of Leipzig but, after participating in the failed 1848 revolution, fled to the United States. In April 1848, he arrived in Cincinnati and opened a pharmacy in the West End, where he remained until moving to Findlay Market. Upon his death in 1890, his sons Edward and Victor—both graduates of Cincinnati College of Pharmacy—took over the business, followed by Victor's sons, Charles and Victor, who ran the drugstore until the early 1960s.[27]

Since German immigrants like Muhlbergs came to the United States with existing skills, many were involved in organizing Cincinnati's first labor unions in the 1850s, headquartered in Over-the-Rhine. At Findlay Market and other downtown markets, labor unions became more important as industrialization and the railroads changed the food supply system. To regulate food quality and pricing, retailers and wholesalers set up protective

The east side of Findlay Market sometime between 1935 and 1943, showing the longstanding Muhlberg pharmacy on the right-hand side. *Courtesy of the Ohio History Connection.*

associations, often along ethnic lines, like the German Butchers Association. Members set agreed-on price points and punished—by boycott and legal action—merchants who did not adhere to them. This was necessary since there were retailers at Findlay Market and other markets who on occasion undercut prices or sold a lesser quality or quantity of an item, seeking to gain a quick profit from an unsuspecting customer. In 1899, Leonard Baehr—who ran a bakery on Findlay Market's square—was sued by the Pillsbury-Washburn Flour Mills Company for selling an inferior flour inside Pillsbury sacks and charging less than wholesalers to attract more buyers. (Leonard was later and more positively known for being the father of Teddy Baehr, a legendary fullback for the University of Cincinnati football team from 1912 to 1915. Legend has it that the team's name—the bearcats—was a play on Teddy's surname as a "baehrcat.")[28]

We should view the actions of men like Leonard Baehr—when he misrepresented his product—with some sympathy. Running a food-related retail business in the 1800s was a hard life, and early Findlay Market had plenty of commercial ventures that lasted for only one or two years. It is an important reminder that even as Over-the-Rhine was then a wealthier immigrant enclave, successful entrepreneurship in commerce remained difficult. In the 1800s, groceries, bakeries, coffee shops, saloons and candy shops at Findlay Market were more short-lived than other commercial ventures, although there were plenty of exceptions—like the Kruse family's grocery, which lasted for decades. A problem for businesses like grocery stores, bakeries, confectioneries and saloons was that there were so many of them, forcing proprietors to drive down their prices to stay competitive.[29]

Shops at the market were mostly family-run, with one to two employees assisting or clerking (there were no self-service shops at this time). Family members expected to work twelve- to fourteen-hour days. Upon starting a business, they purchased—on credit, if they could—initial stock for their store, usually from a wholesaler. For shopkeepers who owned their own storefront, they paid insurance and building upkeep; for those who rented a storefront, they had to make lease payments. The limited size of stands, stalls and storefronts meant that businesses could stock only a limited number of items. Findlay Market's storefronts were mostly less than one thousand square feet, and the markethouse stalls and stands were significantly smaller, making economies of scale—selling many products for low prices like the modern grocery superstore does—impossible in the 1800s. As a result of these hardships, businesses failed, reminding us of the holes in the "rags to riches" part of the American Dream. So many immigrants came from humble beginnings, making it very difficult to gain a leg up once in America. Furthermore, the economic depression of the 1870s—set off by a financial panic in 1873 involving the railroad industry—and another multi-year depression following a financial panic in 1893 further made business difficult.

LIFE ABOVE FINDLAY MARKET: A WOMAN'S WORLD

Above Findlay Market's storefronts—where proprietors, their extended families and other renters resided—nineteenth-century city living was revealed through frequent encounters with birth, sickness and death. Because popular gender ideas prescribed the home as a woman's world, women were tasked with household duties and caring for family members, including children. While women had power in running the home, high death rates and physical difficulties in cities made domesticity difficult. Furthermore, women's lack of agency in the 1800s meant that their bodies endured a lot—continual pregnancy and childbirth—without much respite.

In the 1800s, Over-the-Rhine's homes had no indoor plumbing or electricity. People used gas-powered fixtures for lighting and bituminous coal for heating and cooking, which made walls and floors greasy and sooty. This meant women had to clean them constantly. Everything was done manually, with women hauling water from outside spigots upstairs to do cleaning, laundry and cooking. With no indoor bathrooms, women bathed children in a piecemeal fashion within a large tub. They heated water on cast-iron stoves, filling the bathing vessel. While coal smoke vented through chimney flues, apartments remained smoky. By hand, women washed and dried clothes in their kitchens, in the attic space— where hooks in the walls allowed a clothing line to be stretched—or on roofs. It was also women's job to procure daily food for their households, a task made easier for Findlay Market women. Since food was so expensive at the time and quality not guaranteed, women had to spend considerable energy getting fresh and safe food for their families, especially growing children. A fresh supply of milk was particularly hard to come by.

In addition to these physically demanding daily rituals, women were almost constantly pregnant or nursing, adding to their burden. From 1869 to his death in 1885, German immigrant August Siegmann ran his shoemaking, fitting and binding business within the storefront of 131 West Elder on Findlay Market's square, while he and his family lived upstairs. Siegmann's wife—Elizabeth, an immigrant from Bavaria—had at least eight children when she lived there, one after the next. Women spent most of their adult lives either pregnant or nursing, mainly because pregnancy was difficult to regulate. After the 1873 Comstock Laws criminalized contraception as an obscene material and forbid its distribution through the U.S. Postal Service, women who sought birth control had to rely on an unregulated black market of various devices and substances, some advertised as vaguely as "female pills." While native-born white women's fertility rates fell over the 1800s, immigrant women still had large families, having on average twice as many children as white American-born women. This was due to a variety of cultural and economic factors. A growing middle-class of native-born white women had access to physicians, some of whom sympathetically provided contraception. Immigrant women, conversely, frowned upon going to a male physician and instead relied on advice from female relatives, friends and midwives. While skilled midwives offered valuable advice—for instance, recommending breastfeeding as birth control (which we now know helps to

Interior scenes common to Cincinnati's old basin buildings. Layers of wallpaper covered plaster walls. Wood floors were painted or covered. Decorative woodwork surrounded double-hung wood windows. Cast-iron stoves had flues for venting. Inside space was limited, especially when multiple families resided in apartments above storefronts. Most amenities—like toilets and water access—were outside. *Courtesy of the Public Library of Cincinnati and Hamilton County.*

suppress ovulation)—many immigrant women came from more patriarchal cultures that prevented women from exercising decision-making when it came to sex and reproduction.[30]

A consequence of these realities meant that women had few options if they undesirably became pregnant, especially if they were unmarried. Such was apparent at Findlay Market on March 3, 1874, when a grocer at 104 West Elder—at the northeast end of the market square—heard a baby's cry from behind his building. There, he discovered an infant at the bottom of the privy toilet. The *Enquirer* reported that the newly born infant belonged to a young unmarried woman, Jennie Brown, who insisted that the whole thing was an accident—that she had accidentally dropped the baby there and had not purposefully abandoned it. Regardless of how one feels about her actions, we can get a sense for her desperation, and sadly, she was not unique. Such stories, of women abandoning infants or using privy toilets for abortions, can be found in nineteenth-century newspapers. This was an era when having a child out of wedlock made a woman a social pariah. Furthermore, even though more and more women were working in these years, work for women was chronically underpaid, making it hard as a single woman to support a child.[31]

In the 1800s and early 1900s, most immigrant women in urban America were like Elizabeth Siegmann in that they gave birth at home with the assistance of a midwife. Siegmann used Barbara Becker, a German immigrant from Bavaria who lived near Findlay Market. Immigrants like Siegmann preferred midwives over male physicians for childbirth for a variety of reasons. Women simply preferred having another woman attend them, especially since most midwives could empathize with the experience, being married or widowed and having given birth to numerous children too. Leopoldina Federle—another German midwife who lived right on Findlay Market's square—had eight children herself, only five of whom made it to adulthood. Midwives also brought years of experience with them. They started training very young, often in Europe prior to immigration, and worked into their elderly years, never really retiring. When Federle died in 1914, then in her seventies, she was still working.[32]

Most midwives were first- and second-generation immigrants, allowing immigrant women to select one from a similar ethnic, linguistic or religious background. Siegmann probably chose Becker to deliver her children because Becker spoke German, was Catholic like Siegmann and lived close by. Midwives also charged less than physicians, often allowed installment payments and assisted with household services like cooking, cleaning and caring for older children as the mother rested—all of which made them invaluable to mothers.[33]

Despite midwives' and mothers' best efforts, many children died extremely young, especially if they lived in cities. Nine-month-old Anna Siegmann perished to measles in 1870, dying in her home above her father's shoe store at Findlay Market. The following year, her five-year-old sister, Catharine, was lost to typhoid fever. In 1876, two-year-old Caroline Siegmann died from chicken pox. The next year, Elizabeth lost another child, eight-week-old son Joseph, to "convulsions." Seven-month-old John had fatal meningitis in 1880, and seven-year-old Frank caught the croup in 1881, killing him. Around one-fourth of children born in the late 1800s—and upward of 30 percent in cities—died before they could celebrate their first birthday, succumbing to now curable acute diseases and illnesses.

Death cards for members of the Siegmann family at 131 West Elder (then numbered 67 Elder). The cards show the age of the deceased, their location at death, the cause, the physician who confirmed the death and the burial place. *Courtesy of Ohio Digital Resource Commons, University of Cincinnati.*

Women, then, were expected to mother several children who would never grow up.[34]

Aside from children, adults had significantly shorter lifespans in 1800s urban America, making women's job as family nurturer very difficult. Infectious diseases were poorly understood until the late 1800s, leading many to die from cholera—which ravaged Cincinnati in 1832–33 and 1849—as well as typhus, tuberculosis, typhoid fever, smallpox and others. Not until the turn of the twentieth century did medicine in the United States professionalize, with physicians having to undergo mandatory medical schooling, clinical training, competency boards and state licensing. Until then, people understood that cities were lethal places. Much of the available work—especially industrial jobs—strained bodies, as did the ubiquitous coal smoke hanging around the air. In 1888, Oscar Hoffman, a young man who lived above Findlay Market, died at his place of work, the Cincinnati Ice Company, when he and a colleague fell sixty feet from the dark attic of the storehouse to its cellar, dying immediately from impact.[35]

One final story—of Oscar Hoffman's family—illuminates another dark side to nineteenth-century living: that of violence at home. In 1878, Oscar's father, John Hoffman—a German immigrant who lived in a third-floor apartment in 104 West Elder on the north side of Findlay Market's square—accidentally killed his eldest son, Edward, his favorite child. Hoffman had been cleaning his gun when it went off accidentally. Edward—just before he succumbed to his wounds—insisted that his father was intoxicated and had not meant harm. As a result, John Hoffman did not serve time, but he took to further drinking and began to hate his other son, Robert, Oscar's brother. John Hoffman had worked as a garment cutter but stopped and then deserted his family. His wife, Catherine, to keep the family afloat, began to do sewing work for a tailor.[36]

Around the New Year in 1883, Hoffman—then drinking heavily, unemployed and evicted for nonpayment of rent—went to a police station in Over-the-Rhine, where he claimed that his wife had been unfaithful to him years ago. Police—the same ones who had attended to Hoffman's first murder five years prior—did not believe him. Rebuked, Hoffman went to a nearby saloon, where he brandished a large revolver and said he was going to finish his unfaithful wife with it. Around the same time, Hoffman's daughter Christina went to the same police station, fearing for her and her family's safety in light of her father's worsening behavior. On January 13, 1883, Hoffman, "lurking in the hall-way of the large brick tenement [at 104 West Elder]," shot his son Robert, killing him.[37]

The Hoffmans illuminate how alcohol was a prevalent part of many European immigrant cultures—especially among Germans—to the point that abuse occurred. The temperance movement that developed over the 1800s was especially strong in rural Ohio, and downtown Cincinnati was a focal point for its members because of the large number of breweries and saloons there. In 1893, the per capita consumption of beer nationally was sixteen gallons annually, but in Cincinnati the average per capita consumption was forty gallons per person, two and a half times the national average. Much of this was casual consumption of relatively low-strength lager, but excess did occur, and temperance advocates pointed to men like Hoffman as the reason to prohibit alcohol. Captured in the plight of Hoffman's wife and children, alcohol did lead to waywardness and violence in some men. That fell on the backs of women and children who endured domestic abuse and were forced to take on more work when husbands and fathers spent too much time drinking.[38]

CHAPTER 2

A BUSTLING MARKET

FINDLAY MARKET AT
THE TURN OF THE TWENTIETH CENTURY

J ust before Christmas 1902, the *Cincinnati Enquirer* declared Findlay
Market "the liveliest spot in the City for Genuine Bargains":

> *Ed Romer's new store is rapidly approaching completion, and he is anxious
> to dispose of everything he possibly can in order to reduce expenses. He
> has holiday goods in profusion, and the bargains he is offering in Dry
> Goods, Carpets and Furnishing Goods is simply astonishing. At Hellman's
> Shoe emporium, Mr. Hellman is offering Krippendorf, Dittman & Co.'s
> Fine Ladies shoes, the best shoe made....George Burger, the most reliable
> grocer in the neighborhood, is well stocked with a full line of goods for
> Christmas and ordinary use. The finest poultry and meats are on display
> in F.B. Funke's meat market. The daily consignment of fish and oysters
> by Wm. C. Wits is attracting many customers. John Veser's Sons' display
> of Clothing and Furnishings is unsurpassable. J.I. Stein, the Queensware
> man, is determined not to be undersold. The Muehlberg Pharmacy has
> reduced the price of Cod Liver Coil to 39c.*[39]

Turn-of-the-twentieth-century Findlay Market exhibited an impressive
diversity of fresh products and essential goods and services. The market
and its immediate area served as a key shopping and service area for Over-
the-Rhine, offering people not only fresh meat, poultry, fish, dairy, bread
and produce but also dry goods, tea, coffee, candy, wine, liquor, clothing,
shoes, furniture, hardware, appliances, wallpaper, notions, gifts, chinaware,
pharmaceuticals, lunch spots, saloons and even multiple banks.[40]

Crowded Over-the-Rhine, 1920. The view shows the eastern parts of Over-the-Rhine, east of Findlay Market. (The photo was taken at Peaslee School looking northeast.) *Courtesy of the Public Library of Cincinnati and Hamilton County.*

Aside from Findlay Market, many of the businesses there had storefronts and stalls at other downtown markets. Merchants switched between the spaces since they were not open on the same days. This bustling commercial activity reflected an incredibly dense, lively urban core, a reality for cities across the United States around 1900. Over-the-Rhine, within its 110 blocks, had an astounding 44,475 people then, showing how the turn of the twentieth century was a highpoint for American urbanism. From 1880 to 1900, cities gained an unprecedented 15 million people. While urban areas were heavily polluted and in many places horribly overcrowded, their density reflected a vitality that faded within a few decades.[41]

So much of this economic and cultural energy was driven by large concentrations of immigrants, which was apparent in Cincinnati at Findlay Market. There, immigrants—German-speaking ones in the majority—ran the stalls and storefronts. They were joined by many Jewish newcomers from central and eastern Europe, indicative that Over-the-Rhine was attracting new groups. Women were another major—and newer—group of workers at Findlay Market, revealing the growing number of married and single women in the waged workforce.

In response to unprecedented concentrations of people in cities, municipal governments across the United States instituted a multitude of reforms around 1900, called progressivism, trying to make cities cleaner and safer and their leadership less corrupt. In Cincinnati, the Progressive era resulted in public health changes for its downtown markets. The city, in its ongoing role as market manager, added refrigeration to Findlay's markethouse and enclosed the structure with exterior walls in an effort to improve food quality.

The Progressive era also saw cities planning and zoning for the first time. In those practices, municipal administrators began to view their urban cores with distaste, seeing highly populated immigrant enclaves like Over-the-Rhine as crowded and disorderly. Contributing to this, anti-immigrant feeling in America was growing, further condemning neighborhoods like Over-the-Rhine. As the federal government closed U.S. borders in the 1920s, city leaders simultaneously reconfigured their ideal city to be sprawling and anti-dense, with residences separate from business and industry. With these policy shifts at the federal and local level, the peak of urbanity around 1900 began to recede by 1920, a development that affected even busy Findlay Market.

A MARKET RUN BY IMMIGRANTS: THE ENDURING GERMAN PRESENCE

Between 1880 and 1924, 23.5 million immigrants arrived in the United States in a watershed moment for immigration. The United States had relatively open borders then, and economic and political forces pushed people—largely from central, southern and eastern Europe—to American shores. The country also saw smaller numbers from Mexico, Canada and—prior to the 1882 Chinese Exclusion Act—from China and Japan. Unlike other midwestern cities, Cincinnati's peak immigration—primarily of Germans and Irish—was in the mid-1800s, corresponding to its rise in pork packing, whiskey and other industries. Closer to 1900, many immigrants to the United States chose different cities in the Midwest closer to the Great Lakes—Chicago, Pittsburgh, Cleveland, Detroit—which offered immigrants jobs in steel and iron manufacturing. That said, Cincinnati still continued to attract immigrants. Germans remained the primary foreign-born group, followed by European Jews from Germany, Russia, Poland and Hungary who made up more than 7 percent of the city's residents just before World War I. There were also thousands of Italians, Romanians and Hungarians, followed by smaller numbers of other European groups. Reflective of the larger city, Germans remained the majority at Findlay Market around 1900 but were joined by large numbers of eastern European Jews, contributing to Over-the-Rhine's density and ethnic diversity. Findlay Market operated as a key hub for these immigrant cultures.[42]

By 1900, the earlier waves of Germans—the founding generation at Findlay Market—had moved to hilltop neighborhoods, seeking to escape the crowded basin. Many still ran businesses in the downtown area, but they lived elsewhere. Newer German-speaking immigrants moved into the neighborhood, and at Findlay, they sold meat, poultry, dairy, candy, dry goods and baked goods. They also ran the few saloons at Findlay Market, indicative of how Over-the-Rhine saloonkeepers were overwhelmingly from a German background. Germans founded many of the city's breweries, and around half of their beer production was consumed locally in one of the city's many saloons, restaurants, cafés and biergartens. In contrast to native Anglo-Saxon Protestant culture that believed in temperance, German immigrant culture condoned casual consumption of spirits and beer. Many Germans saw alcohol as a part of routine recreation and a key part of their culture, so they viewed efforts to criminalize alcohol as an attack on their culture and personal liberty.[43]

At Findlay Market's square, 121 West Elder on the south side had a long history of housing German-run saloons. Bavarian immigrant Valentine Kahn was the first, managing a saloon there from 1862 until the early 1890s, followed by another German immigrant, Martin Henz, who operated a saloon in the space until 1899.[44]

Ludwig Seegmueller—another German immigrant—took over the space next with his saloon. Born in 1868 in southern Germany, he immigrated in 1888, worked for Crown Brewery in Over-the-Rhine and then, in 1900, opened his own saloon at the market. With his connection to Crown Brewery, he may have exclusively served its beer at 121 West Elder since it was common for breweries to have a financial stake in certain saloons that then only served that brewery's beer. Over his tenure at Findlay Market, Seegmueller acquired a reputation of doing things his way. He got in trouble twice with Cincinnati Gas and Electric—the local utility company—for "stealing" electricity for his saloon without paying for it. He also assaulted a real estate agent, breaking three of his ribs, and was sued for it. It was noted in the papers that Seegmueller was "a large man."[45]

A common practice among German saloonkeepers was to maintain sitting rooms within their storefronts for German societies, clubs and other social, cultural and fraternal organizations to gather in, something that Seegmueller provided. In this way, the saloons acted like neighborhood clubhouses (*stammlokal*) where men could conduct business, play cards, organize charities and relief and otherwise have a space away from home to socialize. Only men patronized saloons like Seegmueller's, as they were considered inappropriate places for women. That Seegmueller was a large man who would occasionally get into fights reveals how saloons were places of and for a physical male culture.[46]

In 1905, Frederick Jacob Deprez—another German immigrant who came to the United States in the 1880s—became the next saloon proprietor at 121 West Elder, calling his business the Brookfield Hall. There he offered choice wines, liquors and cigars. Beyond its functioning as a saloon, Brookfield Hall also served—like Seegmueller's business had—as a hall for parties, weddings and events and as a meeting space for unions, clubs and mutual aid associations and societies, many of them for German immigrants. Deprez and the other saloonkeepers at 121 West Elder appreciated it being a corner building since such locations allowed Germans to keep their saloons open on Sundays, when alcohol sales were prohibited, while watching for police.[47]

Deprez's successor—German immigrant Christian Sachs—similarly used the saloon as an important social space for such neighborhood unions, societies and clubs. Sachs operated his business from 1910 until 1938, briefly transitioning it to a soft drinks shop during Prohibition in the 1920s.[48]

Sachs was born in 1872 in a small town in northern Bavaria called Burgsinn. Orphaned young, he was raised, along with his younger brother, by his uncle. As times were tough, Sachs worked in a family saloon in Burgsinn, with the hope of eventually owning his own. He emigrated in the summer of 1899, leaving through Hamburg and traveling to Ellis Island in New York City on the *Patricia* steamship, one of the many ships that ran on the *Hamburg-Amerika Linie* between the United States and Germany. Then single, he moved to Cincinnati, where he worked as a *metzgergeselle* (a butcher). In 1903, Sachs married a German immigrant woman, Margaret Schramm, and together they had a son, William.[49]

From butchering, Sachs moved into saloon proprietorship at Findlay Market, and his café was a favorite in German Cincinnati. Sachs himself was known for being a generous and friendly person, further helping draw fellow Germans to the space. His saloon, like Seegmueller's and Depresz's, hosted the weekly and monthly meetings of numerous German cultural

Above: Christian Sachs (1872–1938), *second from right*, in front of his café at 121 West Elder. *Courtesy of Jim Kennedy.*

Left: Christian Sachs seated with his wife, Margaret (1877–1968), and their son William (1903–1993). Christian and Margaret were from different areas of Bavaria, so they did not know each other prior to immigration. Margaret's two sisters, Kunigunda ("Kuni") and Magdalena ("Lena"), immigrated to Cincinnati first, and Kuni thereafter sponsored Margaret's immigration through Ellis Island. *Courtesy of Jim Kennedy.*

clubs and societies like *Druiden Saengerchor*, a German singing choir. On his storefront, Christian advertised the building as a "hall for meetings" and etched *"Druiden Saenger-Chor"* above the windows, signaling his proud use of the space by the German singers. Outside of playing host, Sachs was involved in several of these organizations. He was a member of the German American Citizens League, a patriotic society devoted to maintaining strong German culture for Cincinnati Germans through fun social gatherings like German Day at Coney Island, Cincinnati's main amusement park. For his efforts, Germans often referred to Sachs as "our hostel warden Chris." His beloved café lasted until his death in 1938, when, a few days after Christmas, William Sachs found his father in their car behind the garage of their house, dead from a heart attack.[50]

That Seegmueller, Deprez and Sachs offered space to a variety of German groups speaks to the power of these immigrant institutions, much like the *Deutsche Pionierverein* set up by earlier generations of Germans. By World War I, Cincinnati was supporting well over one hundred different German clubs, associations and societies. Findlay Market's use as a hub for these groups reminds us again of the importance of immigrants there, as merchants, shoppers and residents forming a community.[51]

A MARKET RUN BY IMMIGRANTS: JEWISH MERCHANTS

Aside from Germans, Findlay Market also showed the large proportion of Jewish immigrants—from Germany, Austria, Hungary, Slovenia, Russia, Poland, Romania and Ukraine—in Cincinnati. In this immigration, Cincinnati was not unique. Many Jews came to the United States around the turn of the twentieth century, fleeing heightened persecution in Europe. They overwhelmingly settled in cities. In Cincinnati, indicative of this group's presence, almost 20 percent of the storefronts rimming Findlay Market housed Jewish immigrant–owned businesses in the years around 1900.[52]

European Jews had been coming to Cincinnati since the early 1800s, to the point that Cincinnati had one of the largest Jewish communities in the country in 1850, somewhere between 2,500 and 3,500 people. This early wave of Jewish immigrants was from England, France, Holland and different German states, with smaller numbers from eastern Europe. Many of the early German Jews settled in Over-the-Rhine. Like the non-Jewish Germans there, they founded businesses, supported German cultural institutions, and—as assimilated Americans—got involved in local politics.[53]

Jewish immigration to Cincinnati accelerated in the late 1800s, when many more Jews came from central and eastern Europe due to increasing anti-Semitism there. Oppressive living conditions and a growing number of pogroms—violent attacks on Jewish communities—forced them to leave. Fleeing oppression, these Jewish immigrants were less affluent than the earlier wave of Jewish immigrants. Of those coming to Cincinnati around 1900, many Russian Jews settled in the West End (so many that it became known as a Jewish ghetto), and those from Austria-Hungary and Romania settled in the northern edge of Over-the-Rhine.[54]

Most Jews emigrated from the Pale of Settlement, an area in eastern Europe established by tsarist Russia in the late eighteenth century where Jews were legally authorized to live. There, many lived in cities and towns while others lived in small *shtetls* (the Yiddish word for village) in the rural countryside. In these locations, Jews were forbidden to own land and work in certain professions. With these restrictions, Jews became concentrated in certain permitted artisan trades—like tailoring—as well as commerce. This was evident at Findlay Market in the numerous Jewish shopkeepers in clothing, shoes, dry goods, coffee and tea, chinaware, gifts and notions.

One longstanding Jewish merchant at turn-of-the-century Findlay Market was Gustave Loewenstein, a German Jew. A butcher by trade, Loewenstein got into the dry goods business in the 1890s. At Findlay Market, customers could buy tea, coffee and dry groceries at his Great China Tea Company. By 1900, the company had expanded to thirty-one retail locations, indicative of Loewenstein's success. Born in 1854, Loewenstein had immigrated to the United States in 1870, and in that, he represented the earlier—and more affluent—wave of German Jewish immigrants who came to Cincinnati prior to the turn of the twentieth century. Indicative of this, the Loewensteins— Gustave; his German wife, Rachel (née Bloch); and their children—lived in Walnut Hills and then Avondale, nice neighborhoods with sizeable Jewish populations. As the Germans who founded Findlay Market's first businesses moved to hilltop and farther-out suburbs by the late 1800s, German Jewish families among them similarly migrated out of downtown.[55]

Loewenstein served multiple times in the 1880s on city council, including as its president. That Loewenstein was a Jewish immigrant and a councilmember illustrated the potential political influence that immigrants, including Jewish ones, could have in a major U.S. city around 1900. Furthermore, Loewenstein's entry into politics underscored his belief that— even though anti-Semitism existed in the United States—it was less pervasive than in European states. Taking advantage of religious tolerance and ideas of equality in the United States, Loewenstein followed the footsteps of other German Jews in Cincinnati who, since the mid-1800s, had been elected and appointed to serve in political positions. Cincinnatians elected a German Jew, Julius Fleischmann, as mayor twice, in 1900 and again in 1905.[56]

As a councilmember, Loewenstein was known for his sobriety and affable nature and earned a reputation for being one of the more honest councilmembers, willing to stand up to business interests, including the powerful local street railway company. Even as he was less corrupt than his colleagues, he was still a powerful politician, being a member of the Lincoln Club—the elite local Republican club—and a personal friend of the Ohio governor, Joseph B. Foraker. Foraker, a well-connected lawyer from Cincinnati, won office in 1885. From his friendship with Foraker, Loewenstein—as a butcher—received an exclusive contract to supply meat for the state penitentiary.[57]

Across U.S. cities in the late 1800s, this type of political corruption was common, with local "bosses" using political machines to maintain their party in power. In Cincinnati, the Republican Party—largely in control of city council around the turn of the twentieth century—was aligned with Cincinnati's political boss, George B. Cox, who helped the party gain key votes in various wards (voting districts) that he controlled downtown. Each ward—Findlay Market being in ward 11—had ward officers and precinct captains who helped secure votes for city council and the mayor. Cox himself gained power through his connections with Governor Foraker and with George Moerlein, the son of powerful Over-the-Rhine brewer Christian Moerlein. The Republican Party appealed to many voters in and near the basin for its platform of order, efficiency and (somewhat ironically) anti-corrupt government.[58]

Like other political bosses, Cox and his allies exchanged votes for gifts and favored friends. At Findlay Market, given that the city was in charge of leasing space to vendors, municipal officials rented stalls to Cox's friends, who in turn subleased them to actual vendors at high rates. That profit was sent back to Cox's machine. While hardly democratic, this boss political system appealed to some immigrant voters since they could receive employment, welfare and insurance benefits and other vital aid from the patronage. Furthermore, many immigrant voters in Over-the-Rhine supported the Republican Cox machine since it did not generally promote Sunday closing laws—no alcohol on Sundays—and other temperance measures. Immigrant voters also appreciated Republican efforts to clean up the basin area, which was getting very crowded and built up by 1900. (Women could not vote in local elections until 1894, when they could elect board of education members; beyond that, women's voting in general elections had to wait until the passage of the Nineteenth Amendment in 1920).[59]

Another longstanding Jewish merchant at Findlay Market was Moses Goldsmith. From the 1870s to the early 1900s, Goldsmith sold notions, toys, household goods and men's furnishings from Findlay's market square, utilizing different storefronts over time. Like Loewenstein, he was a German Jew whose family had immigrated to the United States.

Born in 1848 in Cincinnati to German immigrants, Goldsmith started his business as a peddler, selling shoestrings and popcorn around Findlay Market. Goldsmith's roots reflected how many Jewish immigrants in Cincinnati and other U.S. cities started off as peddlers, which makes sense since Jews were concentrated in commerce in Europe. In 1850, one in four Jews in Cincinnati was employed as such, selling jewelry, notions, cigars or stationery that they bought from other Jewish merchants to hawk. For many, they began as "basket peddlers" and then grew their business to a heavy pack of stuff to sell. Then they got a horse and wagon and eventually a dry goods and clothing store. This narrative—from peddler to shop owner—characterized the life of Goldsmith as well as other Jewish merchants at the market, most of whom ran dry goods, notions and clothing stores.[60]

Goldsmith financed his notions store with real estate acquisitions and sales. In doing so, he achieved considerable wealth. When he died in 1912, he was known as the "Cincinnati capitalist" and had one of the largest holdings of buildings in the city. He also collected art, which he bought on his frequent trips to Europe. His collection of "ivories" was thought to be "the finest and most complete in the United States," as the *Enquirer* noted in 1912.[61]

He was also known as a generous—and outlandish—host, regularly hosting people at his large house in Walnut Hills. When Goldsmith and his wife, Lena, held their son's wedding reception there in 1903, they invited local Republican Party elite, including Boss Cox and his right-hand man, August Herrmann. There, as guests arrived, a group of nuns welcomed them, acting as household servants. Suddenly, after guests had settled in, the nuns reappeared, took off their habits and revealed themselves as dancers, not nuns. They went into a "jazzy" routine accompanied by minstrel performers. The night lasted long. Dinner was not even served until after midnight. The next day, word of the party spread. The local Democrat Party used it as evidence of Republicans' debauchery and corruption—which might have been true, but it also showed the clout and connections of Jewish immigrants like Goldsmith and Loewenstein to political powers in Cincinnati.[62]

LOSHINSKY BROS.
629 WEST COURT ST. CANAL 6519Y.   115 W. ELDER STREET CANAL 1195Y.

New Low Price Sale of

Woolens, Silks and Cotton Dress Goods

SILKS

36-in. All-Silk Costume Satin— $2.50 value. A yard...... **$1.29**
36-in. Duchess Satin—$2.00 value. Sale price, a yard., **$1.49**
35-in. Satin Charmeuse—$1.99 value. Sale price, a yard.. **$1.49**
All-Silk Crepe de Chine and Georgette Crepe—40 inches wide. Sale price, a yard........ **$1.25**

WOOLENS

54-in. Serge Suiting—$2.25 value. Sale price, a yard.......... **98c**
42-in. Plaid Skirting—The raze of the season; $2.00 value. Sale price, a yard............ **$1.25**
54-in. All-Wool Velour Plaid—Just the thing you want. A yard.................... **$2.79**
43-in. Tricotine—$2.25 value. A yard **98c**

COTTON GOODS

36-in. Percales—A great variety of colors. A yard.......... **17½c**
Amoskeag Dress Ginghams— Beautiful designs. A yard.... **19c**
32-in. Amoskeag Dress Ginghams—A yard........... **23c**
A Good Soft Finished Muslin— 36 inches wide. A yard...... **15c**
Remnants of Longcloth and Nainsook— 36 inches and 40 inches wide. A yard **19c**

We also have a big variety of material such as Velours, Broadcloth, Fancy Suiting and Spring Coating, Baronet Satin, Fancy Canton Crepe, Silk Linings, Silk-Stripe Shirting, Draperies and Cretonnes, Laces and Embroideries. A visit to us will convince you.

LOSHINSKY BROS.
629 WEST COURT ST. CANAL 6519Y.   115 ELDER STREET FINDLAY MARKET.

TWO STORES

An ad for Loshinsky's at Findlay Market and Court Street Market, as seen in the *Cincinnati Post*, February 17, 1921. *Courtesy of the Public Library of Cincinnati and Hamilton County.*

Jacob Friedman was another longstanding Jewish merchant at Findlay Market who went from peddler to successful store proprietor, selling shoes on the north side of the market and at the Court Street Market. Unlike Goldsmith, though, Friedman was a Hungarian Jew who spoke Yiddish primarily, not German or English. In these ways, he was part of a later wave of Jewish immigrants to U.S. cities.

Born in 1844 in Szilas, Hungary, Friedman and his wife, Lena, two years his junior, immigrated to the United States in the late 1880s with their four children. In Cincinnati, Friedman first worked as a simple peddler selling chicken while the family lived in the West End. By 1904, Friedman had saved enough to start his own shoe store at Findlay Market. The business, at 128–130 West Elder, lasted until 1923, and during its operation, the Friedmans lived above their storefront. Even after the business ended, the family owned the buildings until 1946 (Friedman had purchased one of them from Lena Goldsmith). Jacob's son Abraham, born in 1885 in Hungary prior to the family's immigration, helped his father run the Findlay Market business.[63]

Around Findlay Market, many Jewish proprietors sold clothing. In Cincinnati, the clothing industry—particularly cheap, readymade attire—was prominent, and given Jewish immigrants' concentration in tailoring, approximately one-fourth of the city's Jews worked in the garment industry. During the 1920s and early 1930s, brothers Morris and Hyman Loshinsky underscored this trend with their clothing and dress goods shop on the market, which they ran in conjunction with a shop at Court Street Market. A Jewish immigrant, Morris was born in 1880 in Grodno, now in western Belarus, then a part of the Russian empire. Speaking only Yiddish, he immigrated to the United States in the first years of the twentieth century with his wife, Anna, and members of his extended family. They first went to New York City, where they lived on the Upper East Side with extended family members. Like many other Russian and eastern

European immigrants in New York City, they worked in the garment industry there. During World War I, the family migrated to Cincinnati, where Loshinsky set up his dry goods with his younger brother, Hyman, on West Court Street.[64]

THE RISE OF WOMEN'S WORK AT FINDLAY MARKET

The Loshinsky store was one of many clothing, shoe and tailoring shops at Findlay around 1900. At that time, almost half of the market storefronts were connected to the garment industry. Just across Race Street, the Lorentz Bros. department store took up almost an entire city block. Its stock was provided in part by local clothing, shoe and hat production, much of it made by women's hands. By the turn of the twentieth century, women—single, married, old and young—had entered the workplace, revealed at Findlay Market by the increasing number of women working as salesladies, shop assistants and other junior employees. Across U.S. cities, working women had become a fixture by the early 1900s.

This was a major change. Throughout the 1800s, many Americans believed that a man's place was the public arena in business and politics and that a woman's domain was the home. This meant that women faced an upward battle to enter the workforce as few jobs were available to them. Of course, women of lower economic means had to work and did. Working-class women—especially Irish and free African American women—labored as domestic servants and laundresses. Some worked in textile factories. Women also contributed to family-run businesses. As Findlay Market in its first years shows us, many of the wives and unmarried daughters of German shopkeepers and vendors had assisted running the businesses. But around the turn of the twentieth century, urbanization and industrialization expanded the kinds of work available to women. In cities, factory work in light industry and a growing number of sales and clerical jobs opened up to women.

Even as more women worked, labor was sex-segregated, with men working in managerial and proprietary jobs, heavy industry and skilled trades like carpentry. These jobs were unavailable to women, as want ads made clear. Instead, with production becoming more mechanized and based on an assembly line, employers hired women for specialized tasks considered tedious or "light"—such as painting in a furniture factory or working in a publishing house, folding, sewing and binding books.

Since women were tasked with a particular part of a manufacturing or finishing process, work was considered unskilled, resulting in low wages, seasonal work and frequent layoffs. Men denied women workers access to their trade unions, leading small numbers of women to organize on their own.[65]

While women did occasionally own their business, this was rare. Coverture—the legal status of a married woman, borrowed from English common law—treated married women as total dependents of their husbands, restricting women's rights in the United States for many years. Only in widowhood could many married women control their and their husband's property and assets. At Findlay Market, then, only widows and older, unmarried women owned their own businesses. Instead, the vast majority of women worked for somebody else.[66]

Most visibly at turn-of-the-twentieth-century Findlay Market, women were helpers and salesladies, working in stands, stalls and storefronts. Less visibly, an increasing number of women worked behind or above the market's storefronts, producing clothing, hats and shoes there. They worked in makeshift tailor shops or in their own apartments. While Cincinnati had larger garment factories, much of the city's clothing was produced in small contract shops where immigrant women did the bulk of the labor. At Findlay Market, German immigrant Severin Schwartz had such a tailor shop in his apartment on the second floor of 110 West Elder. It lasted from around 1880 to 1926. He employed numerous women over the years, some of whom boarded at the building as well.[67]

To reach them, he placed advertisements in local newspapers. In 1881, he offered work to "four girls to work by hand and machine on custom pants." In 1889, Schwartz placed another ad for "Finishers: two good on pants." Years later, in 1922, he sought a young lady for a "steady position in ladies and men's furnishing store; one who is willing to learn and can speak German preferred." Schwartz—who owned the building at 110 West Elder—leased the downstairs storefront to various Russian and Polish Jewish immigrant families who ran men's and women's dress shops, linking his different businesses within the garment trade.[68]

Tailor shops like Schwartz's were unregulated since they were literally in people's private homes. Given this, women often worked long hours and in unpleasant conditions. In 1918, the local Consumers' League—an organization dedicated to better working conditions—surveyed Cincinnati's small tailor shops. It concluded that "the majority of tailor shops are under no supervision. Many of them are in private dwellings or tenements." It went on to say, "Many of the workrooms connected with living rooms are used both for cooking and sleeping purposes."[69]

Across U.S. cities, many married women with small children and domestic responsibilities worked at home, where they performed clothing "piecework" or "outwork" in their apartments, in charge of finishing a particular section of a garment. Because so much of clothing work was subdivided—where a person was responsible for sewing a collar or making a sleeve instead of making the whole article—it was considered unskilled and appropriate work for women. At 126 West Elder on Findlay Market's square, German immigrant Emma Bauerle worked in her apartment as a dressmaker, doing outwork for a merchant tailor. Born in Prussia in 1858, she lived at her Findlay Market apartment from the 1890s to 1910, sharing the space with her husband, a cooper who made wooden barrels for a living, and their six children. Three of her children survived childhood, and two of these—her daughters Matilda and Elsie—worked with Bauerle, finishing various parts of clothing. Like all women performing outwork, they were paid by the number of items produced as opposed to a set rate per hour. Workers like Bauerle were encouraged to "sweat"—to produce as much as possible—giving rise to the term "sweatshop labor" and its

A typical sweatshop. Lower East Side, New York City, circa 1908. Conditions at Schwartz's tailor shop would have been similarly cramped, with women performing piecework together. *Courtesy of the Library of Congress.*

association with the garment industry. After New York City and Chicago, Cincinnati ranked third in sweatshop production in 1900.[70]

For their piecework, women's wages varied drastically by contractor, with the work irregular and in the busy season the hours very long. Some women began work as early as four o'clock in the morning and worked until late at night. There were garment finishers who reported earning $1.25 a day, while others said they could earn as little as $0.50 one week and $1.70 the next. This was the case across the United States, where working-class women struggled to afford rents in the urban core neighborhoods they lived in. Density in places like Over-the-Rhine drove up rents. There, a two-room apartment with water, gas and an indoor toilet cost somewhere between $8.50 to $11.00 per month in 1920.[71]

While most tailoring workshops were owned by men, a few women ran their own furnishing shops at Findlay Market. Beginning in 1913, second-generation German immigrant Kathryn Bentz Ludwig maintained such a shop on the north side of the market at 122 West Elder. Born in 1892, she grew up at Findlay Market and worked as a saleslady in her family's bakery there before running her own clothing shop. Even after her marriage, she continued to run the business until her retirement in 1959.[72]

Ludwig was a rare exception to the reality that usually only unmarried women and widows—out of economic necessity—ran their own businesses. Misses S&P's—a longstanding millinery business at Findlay Market—was run by two unmarried women, Josephine "Sophia" Siehl and Amelia Peal, who used the hat-making venture as their livelihood. One of nine children, Siehl was born in Baden in 1854 and immigrated to the United States in 1867 with her parents and siblings. Her elder sister Magdalena, also unmarried, worked for Misses S&P's for most of her life. Peal also did not marry. Born in 1862 in Cincinnati to Prussian parents, Peal lived with her parents as she aged. From the 1880s until 1900, Misses S&P's used an old wood-frame building just to the west of the market at 1803 Elm Street. After the building was demolished—for the current Globe Furniture building—the women moved one building to the north, where their millinery operation remained until the 1930s, ending with Peal's death in 1929 and Siehl's in 1937.[73]

Just to the south of Misses S&P's was widow Rosa Fehr's wine house. For many widows, the death of a spouse meant the loss of significant income and sometimes the inheritance of debt, resulting in women working into old age to support themselves. For Fehr, her husband's death brought her the responsibility of the wine house, which he deeded to her in his will

Rosa (1855–1951) and Franz Fehr (1851–1902) at their wedding in Riegel, Germany, in 1877. After Franz died in 1902, Rosa ran the family wine business until 1908, at which point she sold it and then traveled with her children to Riegel to sell the family property and find her daughter Elizabeth a husband. Elizabeth did find a husband, though not in Germany. In 1913, she wed Harry Arnold Mundhenk (1876–1962), who grew up at Findlay Market across the square from the Fehr wine house. *Courtesy of Tom Wegner.*

along with property he still owned in Germany. However, since he died without debt and with property, Rosa fared better than many widows.

Franz and Rosa were German immigrants. They married in 1877 in Riegel, Germany, and thereafter had two sons, who died within a year of their births. She then had a son, Friederich Wilhelm, in 1882 and a daughter, Elizabeth, in 1884 (who respectively lived to be 96 and 101 years old); another daughter born in 1886 died within a month of her birth. In 1887, the family immigrated to Cincinnati, where Franz—who changed his name to Frank—opened a dye house in the West End. In February 1899, he started a wine shop at Findlay Market. The Fehrs resided above it, along with other immigrant families. In 1902, Franz died suddenly, leaving Rosa to run the wine store. She sold the business in 1908. (Demonstrating the power of proximity and familial connections at Findlay Market, in 1913 Rosa's daughter Elizabeth married Harold A.

Mundhenk, whose family ran a grocery store on the opposite side of the market as the wine house.)[74]

Maas & Springman was another woman- and widow-owned business at Findlay Market around 1900. After Barbara Maas lost her husband, she started a notions shop in Over-the-Rhine in 1885 with her unmarried friend Bertha Springman. They moved it to Findlay Market at the turn of the century. Both women were German immigrants; Maas was born in 1852 and Springman in 1858. They both immigrated in 1881, perhaps together. At Findlay, they rented the storefront at 104 West Elder, on the north side of the market square, and lived together above the shop. In an era of few rights and limited work options, women banded together, as Maas and Springman's partnership shows, forming intimate friendships and partnerships.[75]

The level of attachment between Springman and Maas was apparent in the tragic end of their store. In 1903, Springman traveled to Toledo, Ohio, where she committed suicide at a hotel. Springman had long suffered from chronic anxiety, being of a nervous disposition, and the noise and chaos of the market caused her condition to worsen. Upon Springman's death, Maas confronted the man, Charles Krueck, who ran a fruit stand next to her store. In the midst of Findlay Market shoppers and vendors, she threatened to shoot him. For such a threat, she was summoned to court, and in her trial, she claimed that his "hollering" had killed "[p]oor Miss Springman." "Yes, I have threatened his life," she told the judge, "and if he keeps on I will do what I say!" Refusing to pay a bond of $300, she consented only after her attorney calmed her down and convinced her that it was wise to do so to avoid going to jail. She closed her store thereafter and bought a building one block east of the market, turning it into a boardinghouse—a common way for widowed woman to make a living. She lived there until she sold it in 1922. She died six years later from a heart condition. Indicative of their closeness, she was buried alongside Springman in Cincinnati's German Protestant cemetery.[76]

Maas and Springman's friendship revealed another aspect of public markets' importance for women around the turn of the twentieth century: their use as a social center for women. Unlike men, women had few options outside the home that were considered appropriate places to gather and socialize. Much like work, sociability prior to the 1920s was largely sex-segregated, with men congregating in saloons and billiard rooms and women confined to homes, churches, charitable gatherings and the street itself. In front of and behind their place of residence, women convened to talk, often while working. As an extension of this, "public markets...might

This page: The Mundhenk grocery store at the northeast corner of Findlay Market. George Henri Mundhenk (1824–1886) and Wilhelmina Katherine Mundhenk (1818–1892) emigrated from Hanover, Germany, and started a grocery store at Findlay Market in 1879. Their sons Christian (1850–1891), Arnold (1853–1917) and George Henry (1857–1934) continued it, followed by George Henry's son Harry Arnold, who managed the store until the 1920s. George Henri's eldest son, August Mundhenk (1848–1922), became a famous sculptor, with several statues at Cincinnati's Spring Grove Cemetery attributable to him. *Courtesy of Tom Wegner.*

Women shopping at the Court Street flower market. Markets served as important locations for women's socializing. *Courtesy of the Public Library of Cincinnati and Hamilton County.*

have been called the social centers for the women, as the saloons were for the men," the Better Housing League, a housing reform organization, reflected in 1921.[77]

OVER-THE-RHINE AND FINDLAY MARKET IN THE PROGRESSIVE ERA

Surrounding the bustling market at the turn of the twentieth century was a dense neighborhood that was increasingly working class. Many of the original, more affluent families who had built Findlay Market had left the Cincinnati basin for hilltop suburbs, seeking to escape the congestion of the basin—and to avoid the newer waves of immigrants. The more recent immigrants, including eastern European Jews, were a poorer group on account of their circumstances in Europe. As Over-the-Rhine became more working class, the downtown area, like other city centers, also became more polluted. Heavy coal smoke and industrial toxins lingered in the valley. In an era before city planning and zoning, the downtown had developed into a mixed-use space, with residential, commercial and industrial buildings sitting near one another. This created an exciting, dense city, but one that was very unhealthy, prompting the formation of social reform groups like the Better Housing League. In Cincinnati and in other cities, local government became more regulatory in this turn-of-the-century Progressive era, trying to order and clean up city centers. Among other problems, they targeted unhygienic food markets, many of them located in dense immigrant enclaves.

As earlier generations moved out of Over-the-Rhine in the late 1800s, many sold their buildings to new landlords and developers. In 1914, Louis J. Hauck—the son of famous Cincinnati brewer John Hauck of the Hauck Brewing Company—offloaded four buildings that he owned on Race Street, to the immediate east of Findlay Market. The *Enquirer* called them "tenement properties"—understood to be multi-family units designed to house several working-class families—and went on to say, "This is the second sale of consequence in that section of Race street in the past six weeks and indicates that property there is coming into the market."[78]

Over-the-Rhine remained a key area for investment even as it was terribly polluted and crowded. Among the new wave of building owners, many landlords did not remodel the Civil War–era housing stock that they purchased except "in cases where they partitioned one big room into several smaller ones," as the Better Housing League noted. The partitioning of rooms converted single-family houses into tenements, which better served the housing needs of the neighborhood's working-class families. At Findlay Market, the buildings rimming the markethouse slowly took on more tenants. During the market's first years, three to four families lived within a building. Closer to 1900, upstairs housed five or six families at a time, sometimes more, usually in one- and two-room apartments divided by new partition walls. "Two nice, light rooms, newly painted and papered, to parties without children," read one advertisement in 1882 for a building on the south side of the market. Another ad for the market listed, "Small sleeping room, cheap, by a respectable young man."[79]

Throughout Over-the-Rhine, some developers constructed new buildings—larger tenements and commercial structures—on top of

This page: The dense streetscapes on Elder Street. Looking east toward Vine Street in 1928 and west toward Central Parkway (the old Miami and Erie Canal) in 1929. *Courtesy of Ohio Digital Resource Commons, University of Cincinnati.*

smaller wood-frame houses, indicative that the area remained a key area for investment. In 1896, two furniture manufacturers, Joseph Scheve and George Angert, purchased the two 1850s wood-frame houses at the corner of Elm and Elder Streets, then home to Misses S&P's. They demolished the structures and built a large four-story brick building, designed to house their new furniture store. Throughout Over-the-Rhine, wood-frame rear additions and extensions were also demolished for front masonry portions of buildings to be expanded. On the north side of the market, 108 West Elder was originally a three-and-a-half-story brick building with a wood one-story rear. Around 1900, the rear portion was demolished for the front brick portion to be extended back, taking up the full plot of land.[80]

These changes—especially the construction of larger masonry buildings—built up the neighborhood in a visually striking way, especially for people who had lived there since Over-the-Rhine's beginning. The Muhlberg family pharmacists at 1800 Race Street—the large four-story building to the immediate northeast of the market—commented on the number of people who would ask for upstairs access, to walk to the top of their building to see the city from a high vantage point. People were shocked by the buildings around the market that were similarly four stories tall.[81]

Large tenements buildings enabled more people to crowd in upstairs apartments. A consequence of this density was that living conditions deteriorated. Basic amenities—water, light and space—remained hard to come by. At the turn of the twentieth century, most buildings in Over-the-Rhine still did not have indoor plumbing, so tenants used backyard privies for bathrooms. A small portion of apartment buildings had a bathroom in the basement or on an exterior porch off the rear or side of the building. A further and rarer upgrade was for a hallway toilet, shared by tenants. Fewer than 5 percent of downtown tenements had bathtubs. It was not until the 1920s that most buildings had at least a communal hallway sink, although plenty of downtown buildings still required residents to get water from an outside spigot.[82]

As was the case with limited water access, light and airflow were similarly missing in many of Over-the-Rhine's tenements. With the neighborhood's dense streetscapes of rowhouses, light could not penetrate many interior rooms, making them dark and poorly ventilated. Gas lamps, mounted on interior walls, provided inadequate indoor lighting. Dampness crept in, evidenced by peeling wallpaper, flaking plaster and warped woodwork. Such conditions spread disease, with tuberculosis being a major problem. Infant and child mortality was high. Many babies died from infant diarrhea, often the result of unclean milk. Many working-class women, with work demands, did not breastfeed, and available milk in urban areas like Over-the-Rhine was contaminated with bacteria, spoiled en route from farms and unable to keep in tenement apartments without refrigeration.[83]

Perhaps because the market was an important hub for so many immigrants, Findlay Market's tenements were better maintained than those elsewhere in Over-the-Rhine. Rents ads in the 1920s showed that a few buildings on the market even had private toilets and baths, making them rare finds. As such, families there tended to rent apartments for long periods of time and put effort into keeping up their space. The Better Housing League commented on this trend at Findlay Market, saying, "It is the custom among women in these houses to divide the labor of keeping clean the halls, yard, toilets, attic and cellar, each one religiously living up to her agreement, so the houses are kept unusually clean, without any one person having to shoulder the responsibility." Elsewhere in Over-the-Rhine, expensive but dilapidated apartments forced people to move frequently, "so much that a building which houses two families one week may house four families the next week by changing the room arrangement," the Better Housing League wrote in 1921.[84]

Even as Findlay Market had nicer tenements, the core of Cincinnati was still very polluted and crowded. This same situation confronted cities across the United States, prompting government policymakers and social reformers to take up a number of campaigns to make cities cleaner and less corrupt and people healthier, safer and better citizens. During this Progressive era—the years around 1900—America borrowed ideas from industrializing western Europe and Britain, whose cities were undergoing similar issues. The exchange of solutions showed a unique era of international dialogue and cooperation where social reformers across different nation-states sought out and shared the opinions of technical experts and professionals, seeking to find the best answers to urban problems. It was a time when many in the United States advocated for more state ownership and government intervention in the economy as a way to order the chaos of industrialization.

In Cincinnati, the local Republican Party—in charge through much of the Progressive era—used its power to initiate a broad range of reforms for the city. For one, the city shed its political boss system (Cox retired in 1915), got rid of voting wards and in 1924 instituted citywide proportional voting for city council, with a weak mayor in charge. It created the position of city manager, a nonpartisan civil servant who would see to the efficient running of the city, including the hiring of new city staff through objective civil servant exams.[85]

Aside from tackling corruption, the City of Cincinnati targeted the physical city, hoping to make its dense urban core a healthier space. Cities across the United States created urban planning departments for the first time and inaugurated new zoning rules to separate out where people lived and where they worked. They established parks and invested in expanding water and sewage systems. Cincinnati also instituted new workplace safety laws, like its anti-sweatshop law to regulate at-home garment work among women. While the law did not prohibit Emma Bauerle and other women from doing outwork at home, it did prohibit outside hiring at tailor shops if the tailoring workshop was connected to a living room. To combat unhealthful living conditions at home, Cincinnati, mirroring New York City, created its first building code, requiring for residential buildings four hundred cubic feet of air space for every adult and two hundred cubic feet for every child. Similarly, local code mandated one toilet for two families. (Enforcement of these rules was another thing, sadly). Intense public efforts to reduce infant mortality in Cincinnati saw the creation of safe urban milk supplies and maternity care organizations like the Babies' Milk Fund, located one block north of Findlay Market.[86]

Public markets received their share of attention. In 1912, the City of Cincinnati condemned the Court Street Market for its dire lack of sanitation, demolishing it two years later and leaving only open-air produce stands. For other downtown markets, though, the city invested in their upkeep, trying to make them safer for consumers. In 1901, money was appropriated for repair work on the Sixth Street Market downtown, and in the following year, the city installed rudimentary refrigeration at Findlay Market's main house, helping keep meat safer. The city also enclosed Findlay Market's frame on the north and south sides, ensuring that food inside was better protected from the outside air and contaminants. In 1910, copying other cities, the Cincinnati Board of Health created a new position for its markets, chief food inspector, first filled by Rufus B. Blume. Thereafter, Findlay Market merchants encountered heightened scrutiny, especially of perishables, and were fined by Blume when caught selling adulterated items.[87]

Many merchants at Findlay appreciated the heightened health standards. Others, though, were angered with the changes, seeing the city as a pesky landlord. In 1923, outside produce merchants at Findlay Market came under fire for throwing unsold produce on the streets after market hours, a longstanding practice that had suddenly become intolerable by the city. Merchants also got in trouble for the opposite: for selling older produce— about to go bad—in an effort to avoid waste. At a city council meeting in

The Babies Milk Fund health clinic just north of the market, at the corner of Race Street and McMicken Avenue. With the goal of improving infant and maternal health for Cincinnati's working class, the fund was established in the early 1900s in cooperation with the Pediatric Outpatient Department at the University of Cincinnati's medical college. In addition to this location, there were four other clinics, staffed by volunteer physicians and nurses. By 1920, more than ten thousand working-class and immigrant women were attending one of the locations. *Courtesy of Ohio Digital Resource Commons, University of Cincinnati.*

1923, one merchant told Cincinnati's health commissioner that if not for the public markets, there would be a great loss of valuable food products. "Frequently," he stated, "a car load of fruits or vegetables is shipped into the city that must be disposed of immediately to avoid waste, and the public markets are the only avenues through which these could be sold to the public." In response, the health commissioner retorted, "That is just the point. Cincinnati is being made the dumping ground for vegetables that cannot be sold in other cities. There is no reason why we should permit vegetables to be disposed of on the public markets of Cincinnati that will be so decayed within 24 hours that they are unfit for use."[88]

In 1902, merchants at Findlay Market formed the Findlay Market Improvement Association (FMA). Its purpose was to efficiently promote and coordinate the activities of the market, but it also served to protect merchants

Members of the Findlay Market Association (FMA) in 1930. A tradition of the FMA was the Opening Day Parade for the Reds' baseball team. For many years, FMA members coordinated a procession from Findlay Market to Crosley Field, the baseball field in the West End, until it was demolished. Thereafter, the parade went to the Riverfront Stadium. Today, it goes from Findlay Market to Great American Ballpark. *Courtesy of the Corporation for Findlay Market.*

from the city as their landlord. Operating as a powerful lobbying arm for the market, FMA used its clout to oppose rent hikes for market vendors. Comprising merchants and other local businessmen, FMA was run by a small group of annually elected officers, chosen by citizens who cast their votes at poll stations set up in storefronts rimming the market. Candidates were selected from two tickets—the red, representing businesses inside the market house, and the blue ticket, representing outside stands and storefront businesses. Sometimes, prominent local businessmen ran on a ticket without a direct affiliation with the market. (It was not until the 1970s that women were elected in FMA leadership.) FMA members met monthly to manage the market, using Christian Sachs's café for many years. The association was also charitable—as its Christmas basket giveaway for destitute families showed—and fun, like its annual Coney Island Day showed.[89]

WORLD WAR I: THE BEGINNING OF THE END OF CINCINNATI'S PEAK

In the reform-minded Progressive era, city centers received significant investment. After World War I, people started to question the capital and energy going to the oldest sections of the city.

Part of this was growing anti-immigrant sentiment in the United States. Immigrants primarily lived in old, urban core neighborhoods, and as native-born Americans increasingly disliked foreigners, they came to view

Over-the-Rhine and other inner-city ethnic enclaves negatively. World War I intensified this prejudice, as suddenly German Americans were the wartime enemy. In Cincinnati, German instruction and instructors in local schools—permitted since 1839—were terminated. The city's library system removed materials considered pro-German. Street names were anglicized. In Over-the-Rhine, Bremen Street became Republic Street, and Hamburg Street—a few blocks north of Findlay Market—became Stonewall. Anti-German mob violence occurred, resulting in attacks on innocent German passersby. Federal legislation during World War I echoed this xenophobia. The Espionage Act, for instance, made it a criminal offense to utter words that could aid the enemy or hinder the war effort. After the war, opposition to open immigration persisted, resulting in the passage of very restrictive federal legislation in the early 1920s, effectively closing off America to much of the world until the 1960s.[90]

As the federal government entered an isolationist period, local leaders began to reinvent their cities. Progressive era reforms that saw urban planning, zoning, beautification and key engineering systems implemented undoubtedly had made cities cleaner. But urban cores like Over-the-Rhine remained polluted, crowded and disorganized after World War I. This failure led city administrators to embrace anti-density principles, especially the value of suburban outgrowth. Downtown public markets were not immune to these shifts in city planning, resulting in many across the nation being demolished. These two forces—anti-immigrant xenophobia and anti-density urban planning—profoundly and negatively affected U.S. cities, as Cincinnati's Over-the-Rhine experienced. Even bustling Findlay Market reflected national urban decline.

CHAPTER 3

KEEPING PACE
WITH THE TIMES

THE MARKET AT MIDCENTURY

A t three o'clock in the morning on Tuesday, December 17, 1940, an explosion ripped through Findlay Market when two buildings on the south side of the square—115 and 117 West Elder—collapsed. A dense cloud of smoke full of dust followed the explosion. Then fire broke out. Attending police—who had been on their beat nearby—ran to the market. There, they said the wreckage looked like a scene from the ongoing German blitzkrieg of London. The explosion had pushed apart 115 and 117 West Elder, blowing a cellar door two hundred feet away. Telephone poles had fallen. Wires were strewn about. There was glass and debris all over the market. The south wall of the market house carried scars from the blast, as did all the other nearby buildings.[91]

Both buildings were owned by a longstanding egg and poultry vendor at the market, Joseph Boehnlein. Two men—Joseph Koebbe and Elmer Jack Campbell—used 117 West Elder for their heating appliance shop. Next door, Benjamin Burgin, a Jewish immigrant from Russia, ran a wholesale outlet shop out of 115 West Elder. Several families lived upstairs in both.[92]

The collapse killed fourteen people in total, including Koebbe, Campbell and twelve others who lived in the buildings and were sleeping. Campbell's body was the last to be located. In his death, he left a young wife and a six-month-old daughter.[93]

The explosion was an accident—the result of a gas leak—but it occurred in troubling years, imbuing it with a sinister significance. Through the 1920s and 1930s, Prohibition and the Great Depression hurt Cincinnati's downtown economy, contributing to significant business and population loss. Even more than these developments, outmigration—white flight— doomed Cincinnati's center, as it did to many other urban areas in the United States. Over the twentieth century, people moved from downtowns and old-ring suburbs to farther-out suburbs in large numbers, resulting in the loss of important tax revenue, businesses and people in inner-city neighborhoods like Over-the-Rhine. From 1950 to 2000, Cincinnati went from 500,000 to just over 330,000 residents. After peaking at 44,475 around 1900, Over-the-Rhine had shrunk to 15,000 by 1970 and had become a low-income neighborhood. The federal government subsidized much of this outmigration, and Cincinnati's 1925 and 1948 master plans both emphasized a sprawling, anti-dense city, encouraging residents to leave the urban core.[94]

As Cincinnati lost population, its remaining city markets except Findlay were demolished for highways and parking lots. In 1956, pharmacist Chester Lathrop—who had his drugstore at the market from the 1930s to the 1960s— said, "Findlay Market is an institution. The people of Cincinnati never would let it go." Lathrop was correct—but not because Findlay Market was the only public market with loyal clientele. Rather, its location in Over-the-Rhine helped to save it. Even with its population loss, Over-the-Rhine still had more residents than the other basin neighborhoods, making a public market there a necessity. While not unique to Findlay, its diversity of merchants— many of them second- and third-generation immigrants—drew people, even from suburbs, who craved that old-world feel. Findlay was also adaptable to changing times, evidenced by the fact that a few storefronts housed chain retailers. It continued to offer everyday goods and core services, making it relevant, and it remained accessibly and competitively priced, even as grocery superstores, chain retailers and suburban shopping took over America.[95]

And while these reasons matter, so does the point made by a city planner in the 1950s—that the only reason why Findlay Market was left alone was because it was not in the way of new highway or traffic patterns. The mid-twentieth century was simply an era when city leaders—and many average Americans—saw urban markets and other historic city fabric as obsolete.

FINDLAY MARKET AS THE LAST MARKET STANDING

Across the United States, cities began to lose population after the turn of the twentieth century, exponentially increasing after World War II with suburban sprawl. Most cities experienced this depopulation beginning in the

1930s, but Over-the-Rhine began an economic decline in the 1920s with Prohibition, effective in Cincinnati in 1919.

The Eighteenth Amendment—banning the manufacture, sale and transportation of "intoxicating liquors"—hit Over-the-Rhine particularly hard. Breweries constituted a major neighborhood industry, and by the turn of the twentieth century, they were providing the beer for the city's two thousand saloons. Prohibition caused numerous breweries to close their doors. With its sprawling complex just to the north of Findlay Market, Christian Moerlein, then one of the largest breweries in America, closed in June 1919 and was sold off in 1922. Aside from brewery bankruptcies, Over-the-Rhine suffered a direct loss of jobs at saloons, restaurants, theaters, bowling alleys and other places of entertainment where alcohol was served.[96]

On Findlay Market's square, there were only two bars just prior to Prohibition—Christian Sachs's famous café on the south side and Joseph Heitz's New Deal Café on the north side at 118 West Elder. Heitz's—which had been there since 1897—closed in 1916, unrelated to Prohibition. The tenant who followed Heitz—German immigrant Michael Kraemer—would have liked to run a bar from the storefront, as he had worked as a brewer and saloon proprietor his whole life. But Prohibition forced him to instead sell soda pop and non-alcoholic drinks during his tenure at 118 West Elder, from 1920 to 1924. Sachs also switched to soft drinks until the repeal of Prohibition in 1933.[97]

Nearby, numerous other bars in Over-the-Rhine tried to stay afloat by selling soda, although many continued to sell alcohol discreetly (there were about three thousand speakeasies in Cincinnati during Prohibition). Just to the east of the market, on Race Street, saloon proprietor George Tabar—a German-speaking Hungarian immigrant—ran a soft drinks business. In 1920, he was caught making his own moonshine. After Tabar, Peter Rinthin—a Hungarian immigrant—ran a café out of the same space on Race Street, yet he too was arrested for the possession of liquor. At his arrest, the police entered the storefront and found Rinthin behind the bar. According to the police report, when Rinthin saw police coming, he pushed a button, which turned on a red-light signal in his café's kitchen. This alerted his wife to dispose of their liquor. Police saw her run down a flight of stairs to the basement, throwing the alcohol on a coal pile. Rinthin's café was thereafter padlocked, and he served a short jail sentence.[98]

More so than Prohibition, the Great Depression devastated cities. After the economic crisis hit in 1929, Cincinnati lost 41 percent of its wage-earning jobs over the next four years. Many residents left the city as public services were strapped for tax revenue and resources. Businesses ended, leaving many downtown office and industrial buildings vacant. At Findlay Market, remarkably, only six storefronts suffered from vacancy during the economic downturn. Even for those storefronts, emptiness was fairly temporary, with a new commercial tenant moving in after the last one vacated. During the economic crisis, the city employed men through its welfare and relief program who provided labor for the maintenance of markets, especially the Sixth Street Market, which needed significant work at the time.[99]

But outmigration to suburbs—not Prohibition or the Great Depression— was the major reason why Over-the-Rhine lost thirty thousand people from 1900 to 1970. Cincinnati's earliest hilltop suburbs had attracted affluent families from the neighborhood as early as the mid-1800s. This suburban outgrowth—aided by an expanding streetcar system—only grew after the turn of the century. It occurred throughout urban America where people— overwhelmingly white families—desired to leave crowded, polluted cities for quieter suburbs, which offered families a sense of permanence and stability that cities could not.

Beginning around World War I, the federal government promoted suburban homeownership as "the American way" which, along with the efforts of banks, insurers and realtors, encouraged many middle- and lower-middle-class white families to move to suburbs. Crucial to this was the new Federal Housing Authority (FHA), which, in 1934, began to offer government-insured mortgages with long amortizations and little down payment for new suburban homes. The 1944 GI Bill further encouraged suburban homeownership, offering returning wartime veterans low-interest mortgages and favorable terms for new suburban homes through the Veterans Administration (VA). Finally, the 1956 Federal Aid Highway Act authorized the construction of an extensive highway system, encouraging further outward growth. In suburbs, racial zoning, restrictions and discrimination by public and private actors largely kept many neighborhoods from diverse newcomers, including African Americans.

As residents relocated to suburbs, industry and business moved too. Beginning in the 1920s, industrial enterprises shifted to suburban and rural locations, finding real estate there much less expensive than it was in the heart of cities. This process of deindustrialization occurred across the United States and only grew after World War II. Central business districts similarly suffered the loss of commercial businesses, which left large office buildings and department stores vacant.

Findlay Market's merchants reflected this outward migration. In and prior to the first decades of the twentieth century, the majority of vendors still lived either above their shops or nearby in Over-the-Rhine. By the 1920s and 1930s, most were living in hilltop suburbs—especially Clifton and Corryville—and in even farther-out suburbs like Westwood, Covedale and Cheviot on the west side of the city.[100]

Like the federal government, municipal planners and administrators also encouraged Cincinnati sprawl, creating master plans in 1925 and 1948 that reflected their faith in anti-density. Believing that each section of the city should have a distinct residential, commercial or industrial use, officials hoped to see large sections of the downtown basin depopulated, freeing up land for light manufacturing, offices, parking and highway access to suburbs. These aspirations led to widespread demolition in the mid-twentieth century in the central business district, the West End and Over-the-Rhine.

In the central business district south of Over-the-Rhine, city officials and business interests—with popular voter support—razed numerous historic buildings for new high-rise office towers, a massive new convention center, a new stadium and an extensive network of parking lots and garages. With growing vacancy downtown and the ubiquity of cars, city leaders and property owners realized that places to park produced significant revenue and tax dollars, more than empty buildings. The central business district was further remade by skywalks, overhead walkways between offices, shopping and parking garages, which enabled people to get around downtown without having to walk on a street. In these automobile-friendly ways, city officials encouraged sprawl while still investing in downtown by accommodating commuters and other visitors. Leaders thought they were doing the city a service, reshaping the urban core to be a place you drove to, parked in and left at the end of the workday. In Cincinnati, the Republican Party had dominated local politics for decades, maintaining the majority on city council through the 1960s. Republican councilmembers, many with connections to the local business community, embraced the idea of a modern, anti-dense downtown remade for cars and office commuters.[101]

In the West End, city administrators used federal funds for slum clearance. By the mid-twentieth century, the West End had become an African American neighborhood. Many who lived there resided in old, deteriorated housing, built at the same time as Over-the-Rhine's. City officials viewed the neighborhood as hopelessly "blighted" and a clear case for demolition and new development, what was then called "urban renewal." While the city built federally funded public housing on cleared

A view of the riverfront in 1969, just as the new Riverfront Stadium was being completed. You can see the new freeway, Fort Washington Way, behind the stadium, facilitating traffic in and out of the city. Built in 1958–61, Fort Washington Way required the demolition of an entire neighborhood, including Pearl Street Market, and cut the central business district into two sections. *Courtesy of Duke Energy Archives.*

land for residents, there was a net loss in housing, with new housing not offering enough space for displaced residents. This scenario—where urban renewal primarily occurred in minority neighborhoods and displaced families—was so common throughout the United States that many called urban renewal "Negro removal." City administrators who genuinely cared about preventing displacement were rare, and in Cincinnati, many Republican councilmembers favored a top-down process for urban development, dismissing input by the people being affected.

These attitudes spelled the end of Cincinnati's downtown markets, and from the 1930s to the 1960s, the city demolished them for parking lots and

This page: Overhead walkways in the central business district, connecting people to parking garages, offices and shopping while avoiding the street. *Courtesy of Duke Energy Archives.*

highway access. Findlay was luckily excluded. City leadership saw public markets as inconvenient and obsolete, not producing enough revenue for the city to justify maintaining operations. One city planner commented that street markets were "passing from the picture." As residents—and merchants—moved from the city center, city officials no longer saw the need for so many urban retail markets, especially since there were vacant stands and stalls in the markethouses. With the growing prevalence of at-home refrigeration and the car, more and more Americans switched to weekly bulk-buying at their neighborhood grocery, increasingly a chain grocery with ample parking. The daily purchasing of perishable goods across multiple

Cincinnati's new ninety-five-thousand-square-foot convention center at Elm and Fifth Streets, opened in 1967. The view, which underscores extensive parking downtown, is from Cincinnati's Carew Tower skyscraper, looking west. Behind the convention center, you can see the once highly populated West End, dramatically altered by highways. *Courtesy of Duke Energy Archives.*

street markets was a bygone era, it seemed. So the city used its legal right as owner of the markets to remove them. Leases held with market tenants gave the city manager the authority to close stalls and refund rent. Outside of Cincinnati, other midwestern cities also razed markets, replacing them with highways and parking lots. In large East Coast cities like New York and Washington, D.C., construction of new office and government buildings, respectively, supplanted historic market squares.[102]

In 1934, after failing to upkeep the Lower Market's house on Pearl Street, the city razed it as part of a larger urban renewal scheme for a freeway, Fort Washington Way, that cut east–west through downtown. Demolition displaced more than a dozen merchants. Interior stands had been only half-occupied in its last years, but merchants viewed the vacancy as the city's fault—that the city's failure to upkeep the markethouse had dissuaded businesses from renting there. The city viewed the market's vacancy as par for the course for urban America—that fewer people lived and shopped downtown.[103]

In 1949, the city tore down the 1896 flower markethouse at the Sixth Street Market for a parking lot. The following year, it razed the Jabez Elliot Flower Market for another parking lot. Located on Sixth Street between Plum and Elm Streets, Jabez Elliot had been in operation since 1890 and at 7,200 square feet was one of the nation's largest flower markets. In 1960, the city bulldozed the Sixth Street Market's 1895 baroque butcher house for the Sixth Street approach to Interstate 75. The city had considered demolishing the Sixth Street Market since the 1930s, seeing its upkeep as too expensive to justify. Along with the markethouse, the exterior stalls—111 of them—were also removed, as was the office for the city's market superintendent. Numerous merchants—some of whom had been at the Sixth Street Market for forty or fifty years—were displaced. After merchants protested and supportive customers lobbied city council with a petition showing three thousand signatures in support of the market, the city arranged for twenty-eight fruit and produce merchants to move to George Street nearby. The George Street market, comprising simple, nonpermanent stands, was soon closed as well.[104]

In 1951, a parking lot replaced the large farmers' wholesaler market at Central Avenue and 12th Street, forcing the market down to the riverfront. In 1967, stadium construction along the river displaced it again, forcing the wholesalers to relocate to a location near Lunken Airport about six miles east of downtown. This move—to a decentralized location, convenient for farmers' trucks and customers' cars—occurred in other cities too. As the federal government subsidized highway construction and suburban outgrowth, it also offered federal dollars to states and cities to demolish historic markets and build new facilities outside of urban cores.[105]

By the mid-twentieth century, there was a significant wholesalers' market down by the riverfront, concentrated south of Pearl Street and in between Vine and Central Avenue. In 1946, city planners commissioned a study of it. In it, the market was described as inefficient, outdated and with no "intrinsic value" other than access to railroads. The study commented, "Most of the stores are in old, original buildings constructed for other uses in the city's early days....Streets are narrow, limiting the number of trucks which can be loaded or unloaded." That the riverfront flooded periodically—disastrously in 1937—and that the city considered the riverfront area to be "one of the worst residential slums in the city" hastened city plans to move riverfront markets. Ultimately, the planning commission concluded, "Another location outside the central riverfront...would do just as well." In 1948, the city's master plan called for the riverfront wholesale markets to be demolished, with new facilities to be built in a section of the West End called Kenyon-Barr, located to the immediate west of downtown. The city ultimately did this: it demolished its waterfront wholesalers' market and displaced more than twenty-five thousand African Americans from Kenyon-Barr for a new industrial park there. Only a few wholesalers moved to the new location.[106]

Through this era of widespread demolition, the city left Findlay Market alone. The city's 1925 master plan called for its retention since planners concluded that Findlay Market, unlike the other downtown markets, posed little threat to disrupting traffic or hindering new business. Findlay Market could remain only because it was out of the way, but city officials commented at the time that its "usefulness does not warrant any large expenditures for enlargement or even renewal." Later, in the early 1960s, the city planning commission floated schemes to move Findlay Market westward one or two blocks to accommodate a proposed traffic structure in the northern part of Over-the-Rhine. The plan—which did not come to pass—would have involved considerable demolition of nearby historic fabric to retain and move the markethouse. It underscored that this era—the 1920s to the 1960s—was a low point for urban planning when city officials failed to be stewards for the oldest sections of the city.[107]

Even though Findlay was left alone, the changing times were felt. Longtime merchants recognized the growing importance of parking lots, but also that parking lots were at odds with Findlay Market's historic charm since to create parking near Findlay would mean demolition of nearby old buildings that customers loved. In 1956, Jean Cohen—who ran his father's five and dime shop there—stated as much, saying, "This is a unique shopping center, and it has the old German flavor that made Cincinnati famous. The city should make every effort to retain Findlay Market." Yet he also added, "We are keeping up with the times, too. We've done a lot to solve our parking problem on Saturdays with two lots." That same year, the city commissioned a parking study for different business districts including Findlay's. Citing a deficiency of more than three hundred parking spaces for shoppers, the study recommended a large parking lot to the south of the market, which the city in part implemented. Several buildings came down for it.[108]

If the city's main reason to leave Findlay alone was because it was out of the way, there were a few other reasons too. For one, Over-the-Rhine still held 30,000 people in 1960. Compared to the West End (which fell, due to city designs, from 70,000 to 20,000 by 1980) and the downtown riverfront (where by 1940 only 2,900 people lived), Over-the-Rhine was more of an intact neighborhood in the mid-twentieth century, making demolition less intense there (though still substantial). Findlay Market's cast- and wrought-iron construction also helped to save it—the thought being that it was made durably so it should stay—although plenty of other downtown markets that got demolished were made of metal and stone material too.[109]

In the midcentury, national polls indicated that the majority of Americans supported urban demolition for highway development. Reflective of that, in 1934—years before the Sixth Street Market was torn down for an approach to Interstate 75—Cincinnatians lobbied their council for that highway access to downtown, knowing the market would come down. The *Enquirer* reported, "Residents of 'down the river' suburbs conducted a demonstration in Council chamber yesterday as part of their appeal for construction of the Sixth Street viaduct." But at the same time, the 1959 response to the demolition of the Sixth Street Market for the viaduct—wherein thousands came forward to support the merchants—showed there were still people who cherished historic markets and the dense downtowns in which they developed. That attachment, while not unique to Findlay, definitely helped it survive.[110]

THE NEXT GENERATION OF MARKET MERCHANTS AND RESIDENTS

A key part of people's attachment to urban markets was their cultural diversity—that shopping there reminded them of America's immigrant and ethnic heritage. At Findlay Market, that heritage was cultivated first by European immigrants and, later, in the mid-twentieth century, by midwestern and Appalachian migrants who moved into the neighborhood, becoming business owners and shoppers. In 1957, one suburban shopper expressed their attachment to diversity at the market, saying, "And the languages! In one of the shops that specializes in German foods you can hear a dozen

Midcentury Findlay Market. Despite Over-the-Rhine's shrinking population by the 1960s, the market remained a fixture for many, popular for both nearby residents and suburban shoppers. *Courtesy of the Corporation for Findlay Market.*

different dialects, including Swabian, Bavarian, Platt-deutsch, Banater, Rhineland, and second-generation Cincinnati ('Them's good, lady'). And at the other end of the market, around the corner in Iacobucci's grocery, you can brandish your half-dozen words of Italian." It was immigrants and migrants—and their children and grandchildren—who continued to make Findlay Market appealing.[111]

By the mid-twentieth century, Over-the-Rhine was home to fewer first-generation immigrants than in the past. While the United States had always regulated immigration, it had generally open borders throughout much of the 1800s. In 1882, the federal government enacted unprecedented restrictive immigration legislation with the Chinese Exclusion Act. A response to growing anti-immigrant feeling among white Americans, the act prohibited Chinese immigration for a period of ten years (which was then extended) and barred all Chinese immigrants from naturalized citizenship. Justified on the basis that Chinese were a "different race"—not white enough to be assimilable—this act set the groundwork for additional restrictions based on race. It culminated in the 1924 Immigration Act, which used national quotas to dramatically slow immigration. Granting each nation-state a set number of immigrants—2 percent of the amount tracked in the 1890 census—the law privileged northern Europeans, seen as the whitest and most assimilable, and gave very small quotas for southern and eastern Europeans; it outright barred Asian immigrants. This legislation meant that by the 1930s, 1940s and 1950s, there were significantly fewer first-generation immigrants in urban America, including Over-the-Rhine. It is ironic, then, that as some Cincinnatians supported closing their national borders, others (or perhaps some of the same people) were shopping at Findlay Market, seeking to be around immigrant cultures.[112]

Findlay Market clung to that culture. Into the mid-1900s, the children and grandchildren of first-generation immigrants ran the businesses. As the son of German immigrants, Joseph Elmer Heist was one such merchant. Born in 1886, he grew up in northern Kentucky, where he learned his father's trade selling poultry, at that point from a horse-drawn wagon. In 1938, Heist purchased 106 West Elder on Findlay Market's square for his own poultry business. It continues to this day.[113]

In the interwar years—between World War I and World War II—Cincinnati also became very Appalachian, with people migrating to the city for work opportunities. Poverty and diminishing jobs, including in coal mining, pushed many to leave. One-third of eastern Kentucky emptied out in the 1950s with outmigration. Many—about 375,000 Appalachians by 1950—came to Ohio, settling primarily in Appalachian enclaves in cities. Over-the-Rhine became one of these enclaves as earlier immigrants left. The diverse Appalachian migrants who moved into the neighborhood—some white and some Black; some skilled and college-educated, others quite poor and illiterate—formed the next wave of customers patronizing and keeping Findlay Market afloat.[114]

By the time Appalachians moved into Over-the-Rhine, property there had become even more deteriorated. The nineteenth-century housing stock, while built to last, had nonetheless aged. It required continuing investment, but that upkeep largely did not happen, making property values drop. As earlier, more affluent families left the downtown basin, they took their tax dollars with them, further impoverishing Cincinnati's city center. Positively, these developments made Over-the-Rhine affordable to Appalachians, who moved to cities without many resources.

While most Appalachians did not own homes or businesses within Over-the-Rhine, some did, including at Findlay Market. Kentucky-born Evelyn Jones Manis and her husband, Floyd, had their produce store,

Whitey's Produce, at 115–117 West Elder beginning in 1961 (a new one-story building was constructed at 115–117 West Elder after the original two structures collapsed with the gas explosion in 1940). One of ten children, Evelyn was born to farmers and grew up in Germantown, a small town in Bracken County, Kentucky, along the Ohio River. She moved to Maysville, Kentucky, where she worked as a waitress during World War II. After that, she moved to Cincinnati. There, in 1950, she married Floyd Manis, who was then working as a truck driver. Also from Kentucky, Floyd was raised in a working-class household by his widowed mother, who worked as a laundress to support her children. After Floyd died in 1975, Evelyn continued the Findlay Market produce business until her death in 1999.[115]

Aside from Appalachians, midcentury Findlay Market saw more white native-born midwesterners running businesses, indicative of the national immigration restrictions. There was William Harold Brooks, the proprietor of Elder Café at 128 West Elder from 1941 to 1965. Born in Greensburg, Indiana, in 1911, he moved to the West End of Cincinnati with his parents as a young man. By the time of his Elder Café, he and his wife were living outside the basin—in Norwood—like most other merchants. Across the market, Clarence Blankenburg, born in Bloomington, Indiana, in 1924, had his butcher shop, the Chicago Market Company, at 109 West Elder from the late 1940s (after he served in the army during World War II) until his retirement in 1987. Blankenburg ran the meat shop with his wife, Ruth, an Appalachian from Perry County, Kentucky, who moved to Cincinnati when she was a child.[116]

Even with closed borders, there were still a few first-generation immigrants—refugees in fact—settling in Over-the-Rhine, including at Findlay Market. It was not until after World War II that the United States had a comprehensive refugee program, a way to distinguish them from normal immigrants, and during the war, the country accepted few refugees (particularly German Jews) outside of national quota limits. That changed after the war, when there were millions of displaced persons (DPs) in Europe. From 1948 to 1951, Congress's Displaced Persons Act admitted just over 400,000 DPs. Indicative that the Cold War had begun—the decades-long ideological and military standoff between the Soviet Union and the United States—the legislation welcomed DPs who showed anti-Communist bias. Similarly, the 1953 Refugee Relief Act authorized 214,000 visas over and above existing allocations in the national quota system, with the majority going to refugees fleeing Communism.[117]

A small number of these DPs came to Cincinnati. Private agencies, charities and individuals stepped up to "sponsor" one or more DPs, vouching

Left: John Breiner (1880–1941) at his store in 1937. He sold the first Victrola Record player in Cincinnati, and from that and subsequent sales he became a millionaire prior to the Great Depression. With his wealth, he and his wife were committed to helping immigrants in need, sponsoring and housing many. As German-speakers from Austria-Hungary, he and Anna were also heavily involved in cultural organizations for their specific ethnic immigrant group. *Courtesy of Mike and Beau Breiner.*

Right: Anna Breiner (1888–1956) in front of her store. Anna was the mother of three children, whom she raised at Findlay Market: Anna Frances (Basch) (1910–1940), Gladys (Deak) (1919–1989) and John (1929–1998). *Courtesy of Mike and Beau Breiner.*

that they would not become public charges. Findlay Market dry goods shop owner Anna Breiner did this, herself a first-generation immigrant.

Breiner and her husband, John, had been at Findlay Market since 1913, when they established their shop at 126 West Elder on the north side, selling small furniture, household items like record players, clothing and other goods. They lived above the shop and rented spare rooms to renters. John, a tailor by trade, born in 1880, and Anna, born in 1888, were Germans who emigrated from the Austro-Hungarian empire in 1904. The couple wed in Cincinnati in 1908 and had three children, whom they raised at Findlay Market. Coming from a multiethnic empire, John spoke seven languages, a skill he employed at Findlay Market to make a diversity of customers feel welcome. After he died in 1941, Anna ran the business until her death in 1956.[118]

This page: The outside and inside of the Breiner's dry goods store. *Courtesy of Mike and Beau Breiner.*

Like her husband, Anna felt strongly about assisting immigrants. Over the course of her lifetime, she extended financial and moral support to hundreds of immigrants, helping them settle in Over-the-Rhine. In 1955, Anna enabled the immigration of a twenty-eight-year-old mechanic from Yugoslavia, Alexander Fordor, through the 1953 Refugee Relief Act. She, along with the

Children playing outside the Breiner's store, showing Findlay Market as the center of a lively neighborhood. *Courtesy of Mike and Beau Breiner.*

Tolstoy Foundation, sponsored Forder, helping him get settled. The foundation was set up by Alexandra Tolstaya, the daughter of writer Leo Tolstoy, to help refugees leave the Soviet Union and communist East Bloc countries. Alongside Breiner, other individuals in Cincinnati—including the wife of Mayor Charles P. Taft II—sponsored a refugee through the 1953 act, in Taft's case an Estonian woman, Reet Kasemets.[119]

The following year, with the help of the Lutheran World Federation—another voluntary social agency assisting immigrants—Anna sponsored two Austrian refugees, Jakob and his wife, Ekaterina Dortovic. Anna's renter Johann Dorth was Jakob's brother (with an Americanized version of their family surname), who had immigrated to the United States in 1951 as a refugee and clued Breiner into the Dortovics' plight. Though Germans, the Dortovics were born in Yugoslavia, and like many others who were uprooted along the eastern front during World War II, they fled their home during the war and lived in a DP camp in Austria from 1946 to 1956, waiting to immigrate to America. With the 1953 Refugee Act and necessary assurances of housing and employment from Breiner, the Dortovics came to Cincinnati in 1956, traveling from Bremerhaven, Germany, to New York City. In Cincinnati, the Dortovics lived at 126 West Elder before renting their own apartment.[120]

Another Findlay Market proprietor, pharmacist Chester Lathrop, played a role in helping a Cold War refugee, including bringing them to the market to live. In 1947, Lathrop worked with Ohio congressman William E. Hess to secure the remarkable rescue of twenty-two-year-old Irma Mohaupt, the American-born daughter of German immigrants Adam Mohaupt and his wife, Julia Nagy. Mohaupt and Nagy were Germans born in Beodra, Austria-Hungary (now Serbia). They immigrated to Cincinnati in 1921 and had Irma in 1925. She grew up just south of Findlay Market on Pleasant Street, where many ethnic Germans from Austria-Hungary resided. Prior to World War II, she and her parents traveled back to Beodra but were trapped there when the conflict broke out. In 1944, her father was killed by Russian partisan troops, and Irma was sent to a Soviet work camp, where she remained for three years. She miraculously escaped from it with a young German woman. Together, they made their way to the American consul in Munich, Germany. As letters from Irma reached family, Irma's family in Cincinnati alerted Lathrop to the situation. He eventually succeeded in rescuing Irma and her mother. Thereafter, the Mohaupts lived at Lathrop's building at the northwest corner of Findlay Market.[121]

A MARKET CHANGING WITH THE TIMES

These new families moving into Over-the-Rhine in the mid-twentieth century did not offset the significant population loss of these years, and even Findlay Market showed signs of this depopulation. Beginning in the 1960s—and as early as the 1920s and 1930s for a few buildings—residential upper floors on and near the market were increasingly abandoned. But the market's stalls, stands and storefronts were not empty. That problem would not come until the 1980s and 1990s. Instead, in the midcentury years, Findlay Market's businesses endured.

In the era of downtown demolition and the rise of chain stores, the market stayed relevant by remaining a place to buy essentials. Some of the earlier diversity of businesses had declined, but the market maintained core goods and services. It even had two pharmacies in the post–World War II era: Lathrop's and Muhlberg's. Inside the markethouse, shoppers could still find many varieties of meat, and outside, vendors still offered fresh produce. Many of these items were competitively priced, helping the market keep pace with suburban supermarkets that offered cheap groceries. In these ways, Findlay Market appealed to suburban customers who sought fresh, competitively priced groceries within Findlay's historic charm and remained useful for neighborhood residents, many of whom were low-income by the midcentury. In these years, around one-third of the market's customers came from Over-the-Rhine and the surrounding downtown basin. The market's affordability was key to keeping them coming.[122]

The market showed its relevance and adaptability in another way too—in the new businesses that emerged in the midcentury. Across the storefronts, there were several furniture stores and places selling household items, indicative that American homeownership was growing and that the market had a stake in what Cincinnatians were buying for their houses.

From the mid-1930s to the 1970s, Elmer C. Duerigen's Good Housekeeping Shop—just to the east of the market on Race Street—sold a variety of household supplies, including washers, irons, refrigerators, radios and other electrical equipment. As suburban homeownership became common among a growing middle class, the industry for home goods skyrocketed, especially with the availability of electricity. House designs changed so that by the 1950s, kitchens became the center of the home. Designed for numerous electrical appliances, they were supposed to have very little unused space. Duerigen's store, as well as others like it, targeted housewives as the main consumers, since the new devices were marketed as time-saving tools for busy mothers.[123]

Similarly, midcentury furniture stores at Findlay Market offered homeowners home décor and appliances. At the northwest corner of Elm and Elder across from the market, there was Leugers' Furniture, followed by the Meisel family's Globe Furniture. Across the street, at the southwest corner of Elm and Elder, there was Crown Furniture. Caddy-corner from it was Solway's, which was followed by Leader Furniture. Showing Findlay Market's enduring immigrant culture, these businesses were all operated by immigrant proprietors. Furthermore, they lasted for decades. Each operated out of multiple historic storefronts, with proprietors removing masonry and non-demising walls to transform small commercial spaces into much larger showrooms. The physically larger spaces enabled them to sell a large volume of furniture, which contributed to the businesses' longevity.[124]

Leugers' Furniture—run by George Leugers—occupied two storefronts at 1801–1803 Elm from 1930 until the late 1950s. Born in 1862 in Fuersteneau, Germany (close to the present-day border with Holland), Leugers immigrated in 1881, settling in Over-the-Rhine, where he worked as a cabinetmaker. In 1903, he started his furniture company, which by the 1930s was commanding a spot at Findlay Market. In its early years, the business only sold furniture, but Leugers eventually diversified to rugs, carpets, other floor coverings, radios, refrigerators, ranges and other modern appliances. Leugers ran the business with the help of his son, George. Like most families who owned businesses on the market by the midcentury years, the Leugers did not live above the store but rather outside the city—in Carthage and then Norwood. Leugers opened other stores, including one in Elmwood Place that the family maintained until it caught fire in 1924.[125]

In 1956—nine years after George Leugers died—his children, George and Euphemia, sold their father's store to Harry L. Meisel and his wife, Rose (née Kohn). Born in 1895 in Batesville, Indiana, Harry Meisel grew up in Covington, Kentucky, raised there by his Jewish immigrant parents—Michael, a rag dealer, and his wife, Agnes. Rose, born in Chickasha, Oklahoma, in 1907, was also Jewish; her family had emigrated from Russia. Beginning in the 1930s, the Meisels had an antique shop on East Pearl Street but switched to selling new furniture during World War II as antiques became hard to come by. They then moved into the Leugers' space with their Globe Furniture store. After Meisel passed away in 1972, his son Alvin managed the family business until the 1990s.[126]

Across the street from Globe Furniture, Sol Levine's Crown Furniture Company lasted from the 1930s to the 1970s. Levine—a centenarian who lived from 1900 to 2003—saw a lot in his life. Born in the Russian empire as a Jew, he came to the United States as a small child with his parents, Moses and Anna, and his elder brother, Abraham. As a young man, he got his start by working as a bookkeeper in his father's furniture store, the Levine Furniture Company. By the 1930s, Levine was running two furniture stores: the Bell in the West End and Crown at Findlay Market.[127]

Caddy-corner from Levine's sat Harry Solway's furniture store, which lasted from the 1920s until 1963. A Jewish immigrant, Solway was born in 1898 in Russia, immigrated in 1912 and by 1920 had started a humble furniture store in Cincinnati with just three employees. That same year, he married Anna Hellman, whose sister, Fannie, was married to William Howard Rothenberg, a longtime shoe store proprietor at Findlay Market, indicative of how tight circles were there. As he maintained his large showroom on Findlay's square, Solway also had a consignment shop just north of the market, called the Exchange Store. There, he offered gently used furniture and allowed customers to pay in installments, making his business relevant to the low-income neighborhood in which it sat.[128]

Following Solway's, the space housed another furniture store with Russian Jewish roots, Leader Furniture. Its origin was in another store, run

Left: Leugers' Furniture store at the northwest corner of Elm and Elder Streets, across Elm from the market. (One of John and Anna Breiner's children stands in the foreground.) Solway's Furniture Store can be seen across the street. *Courtesy of Mike and Beau Breiner.*

Below: A view of Findlay Market in the 1970s, showing Globe Furniture at the west end of the market—taking the place of Leugers'. *Courtesy of Cincinnati Preservation Association and University of Cincinnati Libraries.*

by Russian immigrant Morris Karp and his brothers—the Karp Brothers Furniture Company. They had a storefront on West Fifth Street in the central business district. In 1954, William Mallin—a second-generation Russian immigrant and a butcher by training—purchased a share in the Karp brothers' company. Two years later, Mallin purchased the Findlay Market building, which had been home to Solway's. What was Karp Furniture moved to Findlay Market and became Leader Furniture, run by Mallin and then his sons, Gary and Gerald.[129]

THE RISE OF CHAIN STORES

Another trend that signaled that Findlay Market was adaptable to the modern era was the rise of a select number of chain stores there, appearing first in the early 1900s. Across U.S. cities, retail trade in chain stores grew remarkably in the early and mid-twentieth century, with many major downtown stores starting branch locations. At Findlay, the few chain stores there appealed to customers who sought regional or national brands within the market's familiar charm. Chain stores never threatened the market, since the majority of businesses there remained small and independently owned.

In the early and mid-twentieth century, customers found local chains and a few major ones in the market's storefronts. These businesses accustomed themselves to the market by fitting their stock within its small commercial spaces, preserving the density and historic charm around Findlay. Wallingford's—now a major coffee chain company—rented storefronts on the market square in the late 1910s and the 1920s. McAlpin's Department Store had a branch location there in the 1940s and 1950s.

In the early 1900s, Kroger's, now a major national grocery chain, rented Findlay Market storefronts, only later building large supermarkets in suburban locations. In 1905, it acquired Gus Loewenstein's Great China Tea Company and thereafter used different stores on the market square, at 109, 115, 117 and 133 West Elder. The son of German immigrants, Bernard H. Kroger was born in 1860 and grew up in his family's dry goods trade. Their business ended with the financial panic of 1873 and the subsequent economic depression, prompting Kroger to start his own venture as a young man. He first worked as a door-to-door salesman for different tea and coffee companies downtown, but in 1883, he branched out on his own. With his friend and fellow grocery clerk Barney Branagan, he started the Great Western Tea Company, locating it on East Pearl Street. For a time, Kroger went out every day on a wagon to solicit people's orders. First selling only tea and coffee, he soon expanded to other provisions as tea and coffee prices plummeted in the late 1800s. Undercutting his competitors' price points, he grew his stores to thirty by 1900. In 1902, he changed the business' name to the Kroger Grocery and Baking Company. By the time he absorbed Loewenstein's company, Kroger had 119 stores. He then started his own bakery and packinghouse so that his stores had fresh bread and meat departments. In doing so—offering volumes of grocery items at low prices and in one location—he set Kroger's on the path to becoming a modern chain store.[130]

The most notable chain store at Findlay Market was A&P's grocery. From 1929 to the 1970s, it sat to the immediate east of the market, taking up an entire city block at the corner of Race and Elder. Remarkably, A&P's did not detract from the market's business. While it offered a one-stop convenience that was hard to beat, merchants and shoppers knew that A&P's—or any other grocery supermarket—could never replace Findlay Market. People cherished the experience of purchasing high-quality food and goods from the market's independent shops; customers knew that the relationships they built with Findlay's merchants could never be replicated at a place like A&P's. So, the two types of businesses—small market retailers and a major grocery chain—turned out to have a fairly symbiotic relationship at Findlay Market.[131]

A&P's originated in New York City with George Gilman, who converted his father's tanning company, Gilman & Company, to a tea and coffee business in 1859 after his father's death. He named it the Great Atlantic and Pacific Tea Company, or A&P for short. It began as both an in-person store and a mail-order tea and coffee business, later morphing into a company that offered all kinds of groceries. Turning A&P's into a major company, Gilman and his partner, George Huntington Hartford—and later his sons, George and John Hartford—harnessed the power of advertising and recognized the importance of branding, even creating their own products like Eight O'Clock Coffee. In 1912, A&P's opened its first economy store, and by the 1930s, it had more than fifteen thousand stores. Unique to A&P's, the supermarket chain located and maintained stores in urban core neighborhoods like Over-the-Rhine throughout the twentieth century, even as many Americans left city centers.[132]

Chain stores like A&P's revolutionized food supply and consumption. They used physically large stores to sell a significant number of goods while

Acme Hardware on the north side of the market, located there from the 1940s to the 1980s. *Courtesy of Cincinnati Preservation Association and University of Cincinnati Libraries.*

maintaining low prices. To achieve this economy of scale, chains purchased goods—in unprecedented volumes and often at discount—directly from wholesalers, thereby cutting out many other middlemen previously involved in food production. As the scale of purchase grew, suppliers themselves changed, with only large-scale operations able to provide chains adequate volume. Some chains even became their own goods manufacturer. This meant that smaller, family-run businesses were no longer competitive wholesalers. Chains like A&P's also created and used customer data to efficiently close or open locations and to obtain or cancel products. Since the chain stores required customers to pick out their own products, as opposed to a clerk getting them for you, staffing was minimized, further growing margins. For customers across the United States, the emergence of grocery chains—with their cheaper food—was a godsend since food was expensive relative to other goods. The average working-class family in the 1920s devoted one-third of its budget to groceries. At Findlay Market, though, small food retailers remained competitive in pricing with the nearby A&P's, and the two kinds of businesses coexisted because they covered distinct needs.[133]

Two hardware stores at Findlay—both located at 112 West Elder on the north side of the market—underscored what the market uniquely offered, something that no major chain could replace. In the 1920s and 1930s, the storefront was home to Steiner Hardware, run by Catherine Steiner and her brother, Charles. The Steiners had a reputation for never throwing away old stock, believing that a customer might need an odd tool or part. Acme Hardware and Locksmith, family-owned since its establishment in 1933, took over the space in the 1940s and carried on this tradition. It was known for having all the useful devices and appliances a hardware store normally had, but it also offered items very rarely—but occasionally—asked for, such as a set of "buggy jacks" (for a wagon), a "spoke shaver" (used for shaping spokes of wagon wheels) and a left-handed instrument with a large blade for which Acme management did not have a name but knew was occasionally used. Staff there in the 1950s said that someone came in every so often and asked for an old tool that was no longer manufactured. They were the only hardware store in town that had the piece.[134]

An Enduring Tradition

In 1920, two market merchants and longtime officers in the FMA—a butter and eggs store proprietor, Joseph Boehnlein, and Clarence Stegner of Stegner Meats—began a tradition that endures to this day: the annual Findlay Market Reds' Opening Day parade.

From 1869 to 1905, Cincinnati's baseball team, the Reds, held pregame parades and concerts to lure fans to their games, including for Opening Day. In 1907, fans took over the tradition. Boehnlein and Stegner wanted Findlay Market to be involved in these festivities, indicative of how they saw themselves as part of the city. With their own money, the two merchants bought fifty Reds baseball tickets and asked their friends join them in a parade to Crosley Field, the Reds' ballpark. Opened in 1934 on the site of an older ballpark, Crosley Field was located ten blocks to the west of the market at the corner of Findlay Street and Western Avenue in the West End.[135]

Boehnlein and Stegner's efforts in 1920 were successful. For that Opening Day, they rounded up a band, a horse-drawn wagon and fellow merchants at the market, and from there they marched to Crosley Field. On the field, a band played and the Reds were presented with various gifts. By the 1950s, the tradition included the famous Smittie's Band, the official band of the Cincinnati Reds and also known to play at presidential inaugurations and

Top: Findlay Market's Opening Day in 1950. The parade started at Findlay Market, wound north to Findlay Street and then went east to and south on Vine Street and eventually west to Crosley Field in the West End. *Courtesy of Findlay Market Parade.*

Bottom: Crosley Field in 1969 during the final season there. In the background, you can see the dense, historic fabric of the West End—mostly gone today. *Courtesy of Wikipedia.*

with Bob Hope. Smittie's began each Opening Day parade by playing at noon on the west side of Findlay Market. An hour later, happy fans then walked to Crosley. There, Smittie's proceeded onto the field, followed by parade participants who walked to each base. At home base, they presented a floral tribute to the Reds' manager before hoisting the American flag. All the while, "The Star-Spangled Banner" played in the background. Then the game began.[136]

In 1972, Crosley Field was demolished, replaced in 1970 by a new riverfront stadium with more parking and easy access to and from the highways. Crosley's demolition and Riverfront's construction reflected the anti-urban, anti-dense priorities in the midcentury that caused significant demolition of historic fabric and existing communities. Only in the 1960s and 1970s, as deindustrialization and suburbanization continued to draw residents and businesses out of the city, did city government begin to appreciate that a highway metropolis did not inspire people to stay, return or invest in downtown. Findlay Market's Opening Day parade persisted, although it no longer traveled to Crosley Field in the West End but instead went from the market south to the riverfront. Its continuation speaks to the market's enduring appeal. Unlike many historic places in Over-the-Rhine and downtown Cincinnati, Findlay Market persisted through a hard time for urban America.

CHAPTER 4

REAL ESTATE, RESIDENCY AND RACE

FINDLAY MARKET INTO THE LATE TWENTIETH CENTURY

On Friday, July 8, 1960, Martha Holt—the executive board secretary of the Cincinnati branch of the National Association for the Advancement of Colored People (NAACP)—entered Moeller's Dairy Bar at Findlay Market along with three other NAACP officials. Proprietor Anne Moeller, who ran the business with her husband, Robert, refused them service, closing the store after forcing them to leave. Holt and her colleagues subsequently sought a warrant for Moeller's arrest on charges of denying service by reason of race. A little over a month later, Moeller surrendered herself at the downtown police station. The NAACP officials subsequently dropped the charge once Moeller agreed to serve all customers regardless of race.[137]

The episode shows the civil rights movement in action in Cincinnati, illustrating how community leaders and activists attacked institutionalized racism and segregation by insisting that all people, regardless of race, should be served equally at businesses. The moment at Findlay Market also shows how as the downtown basin's population became more African American in the late twentieth century, they became the next generation to frequent Findlay Market's businesses. But African Americans—who were 71 percent of Over-the-Rhine's population by 1990 and 77 percent of the population around Findlay Market—remained largely excluded from business and real estate opportunities at and near the market.[138]

Late twentieth-century Over-the-Rhine showcased what was true throughout the United States: that civil rights progress had stalled. On the

This page: Findlay Market in the 1970s. African Americans from Over-the-Rhine and surrounding areas composed around one-third of shoppers at Findlay Market in the late twentieth century. There were very few merchants or vendors of color though. *Courtesy of Cincinnati Preservation Association and University of Cincinnati Libraries.*

This page and opposite: Scenes from Findlay Market in the 1970s. By then, the market contained both family-run stores, like Elder Poultry and Marion's Fine Foods, and chains like Payless Shoes (seen here at the southwest corner of Elm and Elder Streets). Despite growing vacancy at the market and in Over-the-Rhine, the market remained popular. *Photos by Mike Baum, courtesy of Karen Baum.*

Findlay Market Association officers in the early 1970s. While there was one woman, Judy Roth, there were no people of color. *Courtesy of Archives and Rare Books, University of Cincinnati Libraries.*

one hand, racial inequality had begun to lessen, evident by the fact that the city had its first Black mayor, Theodore M. Berry, in 1972. On the other hand, major inequities persisted in real estate, business, education, voting, housing and employment. The "urban crisis" that struck cities over the twentieth century saw many businesses and white residents leaving for suburbs, while African Americans remained in the inner city. This created a spatially segregated America, with minorities concentrated in underpopulated urban cores. Over-the-Rhine—home to 44,475 around 1900—supported a population just under 10,000 by 1990. At this time, more than one-fourth of the neighborhood's buildings sat vacant. At and around Findlay Market, many buildings went unlisted in city directories for most of the 1990s and early 2000s, indicative of abandonment. This mirrored other cities dealing with the urban crisis: there were more than 100,000 vacant units in New York City by the mid-1970s; 36,000 in Philadelphia; 15,000 in Detroit; 10,000 in St. Louis; and 5,000 in Baltimore.[139]

With the abandonment of city centers by many white residents and businesses, municipal tax bases shrank, resulting in poorly funded public schools, dilapidated real estate and limited business opportunities. Decades of discrimination in employment, education and real estate meant that the majority of African Americans and other minorities in urban cores like Over-the-Rhine did not have access to upward class mobility, including entrepreneurial business opportunities and homeownership. To have a business at Findlay Market remained out of reach for most Over-the-Rhine residents by the 1990s. To own a building near the market was elusive for most residents when, in 1990, Over-the-Rhine's median household income was just $5,000, compared to the city's $21,006 median, and 85 percent of Over-the-Rhine households received food stamps.[140]

During these years of urban decline, Findlay Market's sales declined, though not significantly. Merchants blamed sprawl—that more customers shopped at their suburban supermarket than in downtown Cincinnati. Even with sales decreasing, Findlay endured. But its survival should not eclipse the serious poverty and building deterioration surrounding the market in the late twentieth century. Nor can we ignore that African Americans did not have access to entrepreneurship and ownership opportunities at Findlay, despite shopping there. This racial exclusion was at the heart of cities' problems in the twentieth century.[141]

STOREFRONTS, STALLS AND BUILDINGS: OWNERSHIP AND RACE

In the late twentieth century, few minorities ran businesses or owned buildings at Findlay Market. Among those who did, they were primarily first-generation immigrants from the Middle East and Southeast Asia. Instead, most businesses and property at the market were still owned and managed by second- and third-generation European immigrants and white families from Appalachia and the Midwest—families who had been at the market for decades. These proprietors did not live in Over-the-Rhine but rather in east and west side suburbs of the city.[142]

Dean's Mediterranean Imports—run by Lebanese immigrant Dean Zaidan—was one of the few minority-owned businesses at Findlay Market in the late twentieth century. From Beirut, Zaidan fled Lebanon in the midst of the burgeoning Lebanese civil war, moving to Oman, where he worked briefly in the dietary department of a hospital. There, he met his wife, Cheryl, a Peace Corps volunteer. They moved to Detroit, where Zaidan worked for his uncle's nuts business, and then to Cincinnati, where Cheryl had grown up. At Findlay Market, he started his own business—Dean's Nuts—which soon morphed into Mediterranean Imports at 108 West Elder (run today by his daughter, Kate).[143]

On the opposite side of the market, Vietnamese immigrant Xu Ho ran Saigon Market out of 119–121 West Elder—the site of Christian Sachs's café—beginning in the late 1970s. Xu Ho and his family fled Vietnam following the end of the Vietnam War. They arrived in Cincinnati in the mid-1970s and settled in Norwood, where Xu Ho and his wife, Janet, raised their five children. His extended family from Vietnam—including his mother, his brother and his brother's family—joined him in Cincinnati in 1979. When they first came to Cincinnati, Xu Ho and his wife worked at a local market and delivered *Cincinnati Enquirer* papers, and with that income, they were able to purchase the two buildings on the market, 119 and 121 West Elder, and open Saigon Market. With only a small amount of initial stock, they went to Chicago to purchase more Asian food and supplies for their business. Especially when it opened in the 1970s, Saigon Market was a very rare place in Cincinnati to find Vietnamese, Chinese and Korean foodstuffs.[144]

The Iacobucci family's Italian corner store at Findlay Market reflected how, in the late twentieth century, most of the market remained very European in heritage. In the 1970s, the family transformed the building at the southeast end of the market into their Italian grocery store, offering customers fresh fruits, vegetables and Italian meat, cheeses and pastas until their store closed in 1989. Carmine Iacobucci, born in Sicily in 1896, and his wife, Concetta (née Schira), had three sons, whom they raised in Over-the-Rhine. (The older two—Carmine Jr. and Pat—became famous professional featherweight boxers in the 1940s and 1950s.) The Iacobucci family was very proud of their Italian heritage: Carmine, for example, was for a time in charge of Italian Day at Coney Island.[145]

Aside from these families, most businesses and buildings on the market square remained in the hands of families who had been at the market for decades. The Rothenberg family—proprietors of Rothenberg's Shoes at 116 West Elder on the north side of the square—owned that building along with 114 West Elder from 1941 until 1996. William H. Rothenberg, a Russian Jewish immigrant, started the business after he came to the United States, and his son David continued the store—and ownership of the buildings—after Rothenberg died in 1971. (Showing familial connections at the market, Rothenberg's wife, Fannie, was the sister of Anna Hellman Solway, who married Harry Solway, the furniture store owner at Findlay Market.)[146]

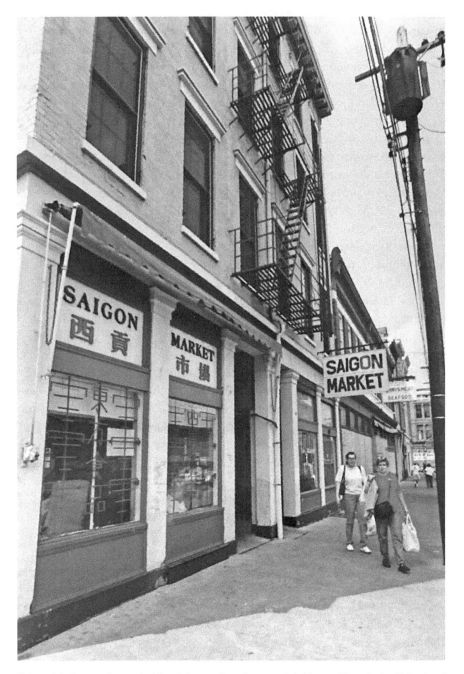

Saigon Market on the south side of the market. *Courtesy of Archives and Rare Books, University of Cincinnati Libraries.*

Various members of the Catanzaro family—who were longstanding fruit merchants at Findlay—owned property around the square while they ran their business from an outside produce stand. Francesco Joseph Catanzaro, a second-generation Sicilian immigrant born in Cincinnati in 1899, launched the family's business at the market with a produce stall. His son Frank and Frank's wife, Mary Anna (Calme), continued the tradition, expanding the original business to a wholesale food distribution company, Frank J. Catanzaro Sons & Daughters, in 1972.[147]

Others totally unconnected to the market owned buildings on the square as investment properties. Master Greek sculptor Eleftherios Karkadoulis and his wife, Mercene—known for bronze statue rehabilitation, including the Tyler Davidson Fountain on Fountain Square—purchased about thirty properties on and near the market in the 1980s. With growing vacancy and dilapidation in Over-the-Rhine, remaining properties were cheap to purchase.[148]

In the late twentieth century, there was a small number of Black-owned businesses near the market. Dorothy Hudson and her daughters, Dorothy Hudson Phipps and Duane Hudson Morgan, ran one—a dry cleaning store, Hudson Brothers Dry Cleaning, just south of the market on Elm Street. Overwhelmingly, though, the market's stalls, stands, storefronts and buildings were white-owned through the end of the twentieth century.[149]

In 1977, city council attempted to disrupt some of this economic segregation by revising laws that governed Findlay's markethouse stalls. Old rules had required that no family could lease more than two stalls at once and that a stall had to be returned to the city once the operator had died. Some families evaded these rules, though, by renewing the stall's lease in the name of a dead family member or a family minor, the result being that one family controlled multiple stalls at once. To diversify ownership, the city created a lottery system for vacant stalls, where the city—and not private parties—would be in charge of sales and transfers. In its new rules, city council also prohibited any person from owning more than ten stalls at once and established penalties for people obscuring real ownership. Existing stall operators did not wholly welcome these changes. Frank Catanzaro—then on the Findlay Market Association—called them "ridiculous." Writing to council, he asked, "How would you like the first 100 qualified names for City Council drawn by lottery?"[150]

The Over-the-Rhine Community Council, representing the neighborhood, and the Cincinnati Black Political Assembly, a civil rights lobbying group, were at the forefront for these changes, hoping to allow for "minorities and others that have been systematically discriminated against" to have access to space at Findlay Market. Unfortunately, these revisions did not pave the way for substantial minority ownership and participation at the market.[151]

A LOW-INCOME RENTER'S MARKET AROUND FINDLAY

Across U.S. cities, a long history of housing and economic discrimination worked to segregate Black families in deteriorating inner-city neighborhoods like Over-the-Rhine, denying them homeownership and business opportunities there. So, as African Americans moved into Over-the-Rhine in the mid-twentieth century, they came not as middle-class homeowners but rather as working-class and lower-income renters with limited options. In the 1950s and 1960s, Black families who wanted to rent apartments at Findlay Market had access only to those advertised for "colored" persons. By the 1970s, after that kind of overt segregation was prohibited, African Americans could choose from apartments throughout Over-the-Rhine. Then, their choices were limited not by racial qualifications on rental ads but by their poverty. By the 1970s and 1980s, most African Americans in Over-the-Rhine were low-income renters who lived in subsidized apartments. By 2000, only 4 percent of neighborhood residents owned their own homes.[152]

Like most midwestern cities, Cincinnati was very segregated, and not by accident. In the 1800s, the city's African American population lived apart from other groups, settling down along the riverfront and along "the Bottoms," a swampy stretch of land near Broadway and Sixth Streets. Later, when African Americans moved to Cincinnati as a part of the Great Migration—when 1.5 million African Americans migrated from the South to northern industrial cities from 1915 to 1940—they settled in the West End. Black families moved to northern cities for employment opportunities and a better life away from the virulent racism and violence of the South. They took advantage of labor shortages from the wars that enabled men of color—and some women—to work in industrial and manufacturing jobs previously unavailable to them. They were, though, always the last hired and first fired.[153]

In the West End, African Americans crowded into old tenement buildings, many without basic amenities like indoor plumbing. The West End housing stock had been built around the same time as Over-the-Rhine's and was increasingly deteriorated throughout the twentieth century as landlords failed to upkeep buildings (they still charged Black families high rents for apartments though).

By 1930, 70 percent of Cincinnati's Black population lived in the basin, and 90 percent of them lived in the West End. This residential segregation mirrored other cities receiving African Americans as part of the Great Migration. Black families moved to Harlem, New York City, and to the "Black Belt" on the south side of Chicago, creating densely populated African American neighborhoods there.[154]

As African Americans moved into cities in the early and mid-twentieth century, white residents left. They took advantage of government-backed mortgages available for new homes and moved to suburbs, bringing their tax dollars with them. At this time, African Americans were denied access to government-backed loans and private loans, instead obtaining mortgages through predatory lenders with high interest rates, short amortizations and drive-by appraisals. Furthermore, most suburbs excluded African Americans and other racial minorities through restrictive covenants, which prohibited certain people and activities in a neighborhood for the sake of property value. After these were declared unconstitutional in 1948, suburban communities refused to accept or build low-income public housing developments in a move to keep suburbs white.[155]

The federal government's Home Owners' Loan Corporation (HOLC) furthered residential segregation, concentrating poverty in inner cities. It was established in the Great Depression to help homeowners at risk or in default to refinance their mortgages at lower interest rates. Its maps, created as guides for realtors and lenders, deemed certain neighborhoods risky for investment based on building age and racial composition. HOLC marked those neighborhoods in red, "redlining" them. In Cincinnati, the local HOLC condemned the downtown basin—Over-the-Rhine, the West End and the central business district—as "blighted" and "declining." This meant, for the growing number of African Americans in the downtown area by the mid-twentieth century, that their likelihood of obtaining a mortgage was highly unlikely, making them renters, not buyers.[156]

The city's view of the West End as blighted led to its destruction. Around and after World War II, large portions of it were demolished for highway construction and "slum clearance," displacing tens of thousands of people and many Black-owned businesses in the process. Some African Americans went to Over-the-Rhine, moving into a predominantly white and Appalachian neighborhood with a declining population. From 1900 to 1960, despite African American in-migration, there was a net loss of fifteen thousand people from the neighborhood, resulting in declining property values and deteriorated housing options. In Over-the-Rhine, African Americans faced

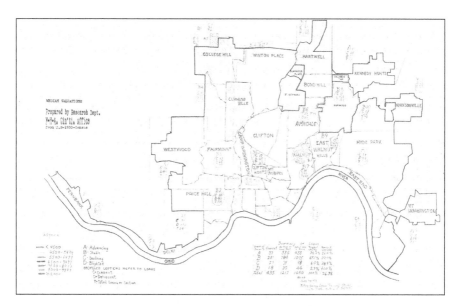

Cincinnati-area redlining map. The map labeled the downtown basin with a "D" for "declining" and listed a number of current and delinquent home loans. *Courtesy of Archives and Rare Books, University of Cincinnati Libraries.*

discrimination in the private rental market, as rental advertisements from around Findlay Market show.[157]

Prior to the Fair Housing Act of 1968, which prohibited individual acts of housing discrimination, many apartments above and around Findlay Market storefronts—including 12 West Elder, 18 West Elder, 118 West Elder, 135 West Elder, 1733 Elm and 216–217 West Elder—were rented exclusively to white individuals. Others—like 1819 Elm, 1735 Elm and 1827 Race—offered apartments exclusively to African American tenants. Advertisements in the *Cincinnati Post* and *Enquirer* clearly stated if the renter had to be white or "colored," although some said "unrestricted." "City—White; elderly, 3 rooms, 2nd [floor], toilet, Findlay Market" was an example from 1958. A good number of the apartment advertisements did not list a price, perhaps in an attempt to disguise overt racial discrimination in price differences.[158]

Local newspapers reveal that both Black and white renters had options throughout Over-the-Rhine. In fact, often a building that was rented solely to white tenants stood next to a building renting only to African American tenants. The difference in renter experience, though, was substantial. One rental ad in 1961—"City-Colored; 2 rooms, $20. Not in teardown area"—captured one of the great differences in the Black renter experience: that your home could be demolished. Furthermore, between races, the quality for the same size of apartment was not the same. Across the United States, rental units available to Black tenants were more expensive on average than those leased to white tenants. Usually, landlords justified high rent prices for African Americans because many lived in densely populated urban neighborhoods where demand for an apartment was high. But even in Over-the-Rhine, where vacancy was rising by the mid-twentieth century, two-room apartments on or near Findlay Market rented on average for twenty-five dollars per month for a white renter and close to thirty dollars per month for an African American tenant.[159]

After the 1968 Fair Housing Act—passed by President Lyndon B. Johnson just a week after the assassination of Martin Luther King Jr.—these kinds of overt forms of housing segregation were prohibited. A response to the ongoing civil rights movement, the act banned racial discrimination in housing sales and renting. It did exempt single-family residences not represented by a real estate agent, though, and lacked important enforcement mechanisms. This meant that local organizations like Cincinnati's Housing Opportunities Made Equal (HOME) had to support Black renters. HOME, for instance, monitored housing discrimination in Cincinnati through the use of hired and volunteer "testers" (white individuals) who inquired about an available house or apartment. That tester was followed by a person of color, asking to buy or rent the same place. If there were disparities in treatment, HOME's legal counsel pursued a case against that landlord, realtor, homeowner or developer.[160]

After the 1968 Fair Housing Act was strengthened over the subsequent decades, it would stand to reason that Over-the-Rhine's residents could live anywhere they wanted in their neighborhood. But unfortunately, their neighborhood did not have that many housing options by these years. While it had been a working-class renter's market since 1900, by the late twentieth century Over-the-Rhine had become a poverty-stricken neighborhood with a shrinking tax base, dwindling public resources and limited employment prospects for its residents. In Over-the-Rhine and other Black inner-city neighborhoods, generations of denied opportunities added up, impoverishing families. By 1990, 60 percent of all occupied units in the neighborhood were government-subsidized low-income ones through Section 8 housing, where tenants paid a small portion of their market-rate rent and federal subsidies went to the landlord to cover the rest. Residents could find ads for these units in local papers. "City—Near Findlay Market, 4 nice rooms, Section 8, adults," read one from 1982.[161]

Section 8 housing grew out of an effort by the federal government to address the lack of homeownership among low-income persons. From 1968 to 1973, the Housing and Urban Development (HUD) Act made federally subsidized mortgages available to low-income buyers. The program ended quickly because many of the mortgages resulted in foreclosures, something common throughout Over-the-Rhine. The issue was discrimination: low-income homeowners got government-backed loans through predatory lenders who charged high interest rates and high front-end fees. Since these individuals were already on low or fixed incomes, they often defaulted. After the federal government suspended the program, it turned to Section 8 housing.[162]

Around Findlay Market, there was a significant amount of Section 8 housing, owned by Thomas Denhart and his company, Hart Realty. In 2000, he held more than 1,500 low-income units across the city, most of them in Over-the-Rhine. Several of his apartments were clustered just south of Findlay Market along Race, Pleasant and Elm Streets. He also owned several buildings on Race Street just east of the market. Denhart, born in 1930, grew up in Over-the-Rhine (his father had a candy business there) and began to purchase property there in 1947. With the advent of HUD in the 1960s, Denhart took advantage of federally backed, long-term loans available to developers willing to build low-income housing, with HUD subsidizing the majority of rent per tenant. Denhart, along with his brother Norbert and their investors, purchased a significant number of Over-the-Rhine properties and used the Section 8 program to turn rental profits into competitive returns, collecting millions in federal subsidies each year.[163]

Denhart maintained that he genuinely cared about the neighborhood and his tenants—something many in Over-the-Rhine, including his tenants, disagreed with. "The type of housing he's had has been deteriorating in our neighborhood," one of his tenants said in 2001. "When you overpopulate a neighborhood [with Section 8 housing], you set it up for failure." Denhart did keep his buildings from falling down, but the minimal improvements he made to Over-the-Rhine historic buildings left much to be desired. Instead of abating hazards like lead paint, he covered up lead-painted walls and ceilings with drywall and installed dropped ceilings. Over wood floors he laid asbestos-lined floor tiles. He cut up historic floor layouts and erected new partition walls to create more rooms in an apartment, thereby increasing the density of renters.[164]

In 2001, Denhart divested from many of his properties. Like all landlords under the Section 8 Housing Assistance Program (HAP), Denhart had to justify rents to HUD. In the late 1990s, changes in the federal government resulted in reassessed market-rate rents, and

Denhart's were found to be around one-third higher than true market-rate value. Denhart had to either recommit to affordable housing for thirty years—with HUD agreeing to only one-year rent payment contracts—or he could sell his housing stock. He decided to sell, especially after the Section 8 program shifted to vouchers. With these, qualifying residents received vouchers that they could use wherever would accept them. Vouchers in hand, many residents in Over-the-Rhine left Denhart's buildings—and left Over-the-Rhine. Looking for better housing, they moved to other predominantly Black neighborhoods outside of the basin. Around 1,000 apartments units were left vacant. Then, with racial unrest in April 2001 following a police shooting of a young African American man, more residents left Over-the-Rhine in the early 2000s. This prompted Denhart to file for bankruptcy for 201 buildings and 1,089 apartments, then 60 to 70 percent occupied with Section 8 and the rest already vacant. As these buildings were sold with HUD approval, most private developers kept the vacant buildings empty; for others, where new owners planned future development, existing Section 8 tenants were allowed to stay under HUD rules.[165]

At this point, the neighborhood was in a bad state: about one-fourth of its buildings sat vacant, and the vast majority of the occupied units were devoted to households earning 30 percent or less of the area's average median income (AMI). In 2002, 90 percent—3,235 units out of 3,594 occupied homes in Over-the-Rhine—were affordable to people in this income bracket, an outstanding level of poverty.[166]

That Over-the-Rhine's poor housing options and physical deterioration drove out Section 8 tenants in the early 2000s is worthy of a pause, showing us a true low point for Cincinnati's urban core. Through this nadir, Findlay Market adjusted to the declining wealth of Over-the-Rhine. New kinds of businesses moved in, catering to families on lower budgets. Around the market square, there were discount stores, mini-marts and even fast food. There were several beauty goods shops too. 1802 Race Street, just north and east of the market, housed a Goldstar Chili's in the 1990s, home to a brief visit by President Clinton in 1998. Many longstanding small food retailers remained affordably priced, helpful to low-income residents. Beyond that, several merchants accepted the Supplemental Nutrition Assistance Program—commonly known as food stamps—including Paul Witte's poultry store, Mueller's Meat Market and Whitey's produce market. (Unfortunately, as a federal investigation in 1977 revealed, these vendors had also been illegally reselling food stamps at a profit.)[167]

Findlay Market in the 1990s. The image looks west toward Globe Furniture. To its left, the old Crown Furniture building at this point housed a mini mart that accepted food stamps. *Courtesy of Archives and Rare Books, University of Cincinnati Libraries.*

Findlay Market in the 1990s, looking south from Race Street. By the late twentieth century, discount stores, mini-marts, fast food and beauty supply shops—like Cee Kay Goods, seen on the corner—moved into Findlay Market, catering to changing neighborhood needs. *Courtesy of Archives and Rare Books, University of Cincinnati Libraries.*

To the east of the market, at 1730–1740 Race Street, the A&P grocery store there closed in the late 1970s but thereafter became an IGA grocery until 1995, then a Shop-N-Save until 1999 and then, in 2000, Finley's Supermarket. These supermarkets offered Over-the-Rhine's low-income residents accessibly priced groceries. In 2001, Our Daily Bread, a nonprofit soup kitchen founded by a neighborhood woman, Ruth "Cookie" Vogelpohl, moved into the space. This trajectory—from grocery store to soup kitchen— showed the ongoing impoverishment of the area around Findlay and how the businesses in and around the market tried to meet the neighborhood's changing needs.[168]

NINETEENTH-CENTURY BUILDINGS IN THE LATE TWENTIETH CENTURY

Reflective of Cincinnati's depopulation and inner-city poverty, storefronts and apartments in Over-the-Rhine began to suffer from vacancy and deterioration in the 1960s, peaking in the 1990s and early 2000s. In 1995, 647 out of the 3,021 parcels in Over-the-Rhine were listed as vacant or abandoned. Many of these were concentrated around Findlay Market, showing that even the city's beloved market was not immune to these urban problems. While the mainstays at the market continued to attract customers and while the markethouse was never vacant, by 2000 around one-fourth of the market's storefronts sat vacant. Upper floors were similarly empty. With the vacancy, many of the old buildings surrounding the market fell into serious disrepair. Customers noticed. One shopper wrote to Mayor Charlie Luken in 1985, saying, "Even though the city owns Findlay Market and is taking care of it, the buildings surrounding the market area have been continuously eroded by what seems to be absentee owners/landlords…these buildings are seemingly bare of tenants."[169]

Beginning in the 1960s and 1970s—and sometimes as early as the 1920s and 1930s—apartments above the market became vacant. The ones that retained residents required continual upkeep, as old buildings do. Instead of making their buildings fire-safe, modern with adequate amenities and free from hazards like lead paint, mold and rats, landlords failed to do this necessary property management. In 1986, at 110 West Elder on the north side of the market, a one-year-old was seriously lead-poisoned by plaster paint chips falling from the walls and ceiling. The health department ordered the owner to abate the issue, but with costs tallying to $10,000 and the unit

Cohen's Shoes at the corner of Race and Elder Streets, circa 1970. Run by Jewish immigrant Abraham Cohen (1884–1951) and later his daughter and son-in-law, it lasted from 1932 to the turn of the twenty-first century, even surviving bankruptcy in the 1960s. While the market looks busy in the photo, fewer people lived at the market then, indicated by Cohen's vacant upper floors, where apartments had been empty since the 1930s. *Courtesy of Cincinnati Preservation Association and University of Cincinnati Libraries.*

renting for only $125 per month, the landlord could not afford the repairs. He tried without success to evict the mother and her five children who were living there as a way to prevent any additional negative health consequences to the children, but the family remained living there for two more years until 1988, when the city condemned the building. The city's health department stepped in, finding the family a new home.[170]

Findlay Market's physical deterioration was also evident in the growing number of house fires around the square. In 1968, 124 West Elder, on the north side of the market, caught fire, resulting in the deaths of two children. On the south side of the market, 129 West Elder—vacant upstairs since the early 1960s and vacant downstairs since the early 1980s—caught fire in 1995, resulting in injury to an attending fireman.[171]

As Over-the-Rhine lost population and grew in vacancy and disrepair, it became synonymous with drugs and crime for the rest of Cincinnati, as was the case for minority-occupied, urban core neighborhoods across the United States. People's perception of the inner city as dangerous was unfortunately often confirmed. By the late twentieth century, Over-the-Rhine had the highest number of violent crimes in the city, with more than eight hundred

This page and opposite: Scenes from Findlay Market in the 1990s. Several storefronts have been boarded up, reflecting that by this time around one-fourth of the commercial spaces were unused. Upstairs apartments, as the floors above Paul Witte's poultry shop on the south side show, are similarly empty. In 2000, only eight people—across thirty-three large multi-unit buildings—lived above the market square. *Courtesy of Cincinnati Preservation Association and University of Cincinnati Libraries.*

The southwest side of the market in the 1970s. The large corner building at 119–121 West Elder—previously Sachs's Café—sat vacant through most of the 1970s until Saigon Market moved in. Crown Furniture sat across Elm Street, as seen in the background, then home to a state liquor store. *Courtesy of Cincinnati Preservation Association and University of Cincinnati Libraries.*

reported in 1993. On the market's east side, at Race and Elder, police recorded more than one hundred vice arrests in 1997, ranging from heroin possession to rape.[172]

Certain places around the market added to this perception. Elder Café on the north side of the market—originally started by William Harold Brooks in 1941 as a popular and respectable lunch spot—had by the late twentieth century earned a rough reputation for drugs, crime and rowdiness. In February 1999, Hamilton County Common Pleas Court ordered Elder Café to close after the city and the Ohio attorney general's office declared it a public nuisance. It had most recently been the site of a murder in January 1999 along with several drug busts. Its manager, Jerome J. Grogan, tried to get it reopened but was unsuccessful.[173]

Similarly, Evans Café—at 107 West Elder, on the south side of the market from the late 1950s to the mid-1980s—had become a place where people drank too late and got into brawls. "The first drunk of the morning emerges from Evans Café, bloodshot, long in the face," *Cincinnati Post* reporter Lew Moores wrote of the café. "The door to Evans Café opens, freeing a blast of hot, beery air." Beyond a rough clientele, Evans had a manager, Esther Evans, who in 1970 shot and killed her ex-husband in her apartment above the café. Then, in 1974, a seventy-year-old woman, ejected from the café, returned the next day, firing four shots at Evans and wounding one man. In 1976, trouble continued there when two young people who lived above Evans Café were involved in the torture and murder of a woman in the West End. By its grotesque and tragic nature, the story received a ton of local press coverage, including that the two offenders lived at Findlay Market. Then, in 1980, 107 West Elder was the site of a deadly shooting. By 1984, city police and the vice squad were actively working to not renew Evans's liquor permit. The café closed its doors at the decade's end, and the storefront at 107 West Elder sat vacant until 2018.[174]

These kinds of stories reflect that crime had risen in inner cities, including Cincinnati's, by the late twentieth century. Drug use had been declining in cities but rose considerably beginning in the mid-1980s, when cocaine poured into the poorest neighborhoods of U.S. cities and was sold as highly addictive crack cocaine. This influx of drugs coincided with existing inner-city poverty. Selling drugs, then, became a job for some. The 1986 and 1988 Anti-Drug Use Acts, passed to combat the "crack epidemic," stipulated mandatory sentencing even for first-time offenses and emphasized punishment over rehabilitation. In their severity, these acts initiated the mass incarceration of African Americans, particularly young Black men, that we have today. As of 2016, 45 percent of those incarcerated were African American, despite being only 13 percent of the population.[175]

THE RIOTS OF THE 1960S AND 2001

These enduring issues of racial inequality and poverty sparked widespread civil unrest in cities in the 1960s. Cincinnati experienced riots in 1967 after the arrest of an African American man, Peter Frakes, who was protesting the conviction of another Black man, Posteal Laskey. Laskey was convicted by an all-white jury for the murder of a white woman. After Frakes was arrested in Avondale, a predominantly Black neighborhood north of the city, four days of unrest broke out, with participants causing significant property damage in the neighborhood. Ohio National Guardsmen were called in as 1,500 people took to the streets. The following year, in 1968, riots in the city broke out again following Martin Luther King Jr.'s assassination. While ongoing racial discrimination and police brutality caused the 1960s riots, so did anger over poverty and inferior housing. In fact, epitomized in the chant, "Rats cause riots!" many African American protesters in the 1960s complained specifically of rats infesting inner cities, indicative of public and private disinvestment in those places.[176]

Cincinnati again experienced riots in 2001, known then and today as *the* race riots, even though the city had endured many other years of civil and racial protests, including in 1829, 1836, 1841, 1884, 1967 and 1968. On April 7, 2001, an unarmed Black teenager, Timothy Thomas, was shot and killed by Cincinnati policeman Stephen Roach in Over-the-Rhine, five blocks south of Findlay Market on Republic Street. Thomas had been wanted by police for minor misdemeanors, mostly traffic violations. His murder—the fifteenth killing of an African American person by the police within the past five years—sparked demonstrations, particularly in Over-the-Rhine, for three nights until a city curfew was enacted by Mayor Charlie Luken.[177]

The 2001 racial unrest emerged out of anger over police violence toward African Americans. But the protests—centered in Over-the-Rhine—also grew from the fact that, for decades, the majority of the neighborhood's population had been segregated in a neighborhood devoid of resources and opportunities.

CHAPTER 5

THE INVOLVED CITY

FINDLAY MARKET AT THE TURN OF THE TWENTY-FIRST CENTURY

October 29, 2002. An estimated crowd of 100,000 gathered at Findlay Market Square today to celebrate the 150th anniversary of Cincinnati's most historic retail district. Highlighted by the 10th Annual "Taste of Findlay Market," the anniversary gala capped off a full week of festivities celebrating the vital role the Market has played in revitalizing Cincinnati's inner-city and in bringing all of the Tri-State back downtown.[178]

This was the city's hope for 2002, envisioned in 1995. On Saturday, October 5, 2002—the actual day of the 150th anniversary—crowds did gather at the market, with Mayor Charlie Luken and Senator Mike DeWine in attendance. "It's a new day for Over-the-Rhine. Nothing is more representative of the rebirth of Cincinnati than the revitalization of the market," Luken told onlookers. The market was packed, although not to the point of 100,000 people. Still, that city officials—in 1995, when Over-the-Rhine's population had never been lower—envisioned a successful market there only a few years later shows the city as an activist and advocate for the market, the neighborhood and the downtown core.[179]

Since Findlay Market's creation in 1852, the city owned, managed and maintained it, as it did for its other public markets. It invested in Findlay's upkeep and sanitation around the turn of the twentieth century, but for several decades thereafter, city officials took a backseat to municipal management of downtown markets. Following a low point for city stewardship—when the city divested from its center and the neighborhood around Findlay became very poor—the city began to reimagine its urban planning in the 1960s and 1970s. A new generation of city employees saw that the urban core needed massive public and private reinvestment and that the city should take charge of coordinating that revival. City leaders hoped that through economic development and historic preservation, the basin could reattract businesses and people, becoming a dense, mixed-income area. Rather than making the process a top-down one, city employees learned from the civil rights movement that they should involve and listen to community residents and organizations in downtown redevelopment decisions.

As the city underwent these shifts in attitude, it used federal anti-poverty funds to renovate Findlay Market in the 1970s. Officials thought that its rehabilitation as a neighborhood cornerstone would spur economic development in the rest of Over-the-Rhine. Unfortunately, despite the city's efforts to stimulate historic preservation and redevelopment there in the 1970s and 1980s, Over-the-Rhine remained very poor and saw even more population loss. By the end of the twenty-first century, then, the city revamped its strategies for downtown revitalization, creating economic incentives for private developers and forming public-private partnerships to see the urban core redeveloped. City officials also provided funds for neighborhood improvement and empowerment, illustrative of many civil servants' commitment to the voices of everyday residents. For Findlay Market, city officials renovated the markethouse again. The city also obtained and stabilized a number of vacant buildings on and near the market and planned for a market district that included market-rate apartments, affordable housing, new businesses alongside old ones and a diversity of merchants, customers and residents. By the turn of the twenty-first century, the city had invested more money per square foot at Findlay Market than anywhere else in the city.[180]

These actions displayed a local government that believed that its downtown core was salvageable through public and private investment and that by bringing people and businesses back to it, the rest of Cincinnati would greatly benefit. Hardly unique to Cincinnati, civil servants in many other cities demonstrated similar commitments, beginning in the 1960s, to tackling to urban poverty, environmental degradation and loss of people and jobs in the city center. In trying their best to solve these complex problems, municipal leaders in Cincinnati and elsewhere often ended up with half-solutions or imperfect results. In Cincinnati, the city's public-private reinvestment in the downtown area troubled some who saw that existing low-income residents might be displaced from the area. They felt the city's interest in community participation was disingenuous. Others—especially Findlay Market businesses—felt the city's ongoing work was worthy of praise but that much more work remained to uplift Over-the-Rhine. Visceral debates that began in the neighborhood in the 1960s—at their heart, about who holds power in a city—persisted through the turn of the twenty-first century and continue to this day.

THE INVOLVED CITY: FINDLAY MARKET AND OVER-THE-RHINE FROM THE 1960S TO THE 1980S

By the 1960s, Cincinnati's urban crisis—its downtown poverty and population loss—confronted city leaders. This was the case across the United States. Inner-city neighborhoods in downtown areas were so impoverished that the federal government under President Lyndon B. Johnson launched a War on Poverty, sending federal funds to cities to address deteriorated housing, poor sanitation and inadequate healthcare and food access. In Cincinnati, city council members and city employees used these federal funds to help existing low-income residents in downtown neighborhoods like Over-the-Rhine. But local officials did not want to merely put a bandage on inner-city poverty— they wanted to solve it by making Over-the-Rhine into an integrated, mixed-income neighborhood, bringing different people and businesses back to the city center, especially to the Findlay Market area.

To do this, they took cues from a growing historic preservation movement that encouraged adaptive reuse for old buildings. With the gradual realization that historic preservation could be a moneymaker—that it could reattract people and businesses back to the urban core—the city slowly moved away from widespread demolition. The civil rights movement also instilled in municipal leaders a respect for more community involvement in public decision-making, including how to renovate downtown. In many northern cities by the 1960s, women and minorities like African Americans worked for and were elected to city government for the first time. That growing diversity of city employees and leaders created a new, more liberal wave of leaders that fostered more equitable decisions in city planning, especially considering that planning had long been dominated by white men.

These changes meant that by the 1960s, civil servants were moving away from blanket demolition of buildings and neighborhoods and were becoming more sensitive to displacement. We remember these decades— the 1960s and the 1970s—as an era of widespread liberal social activism on the part of everyday citizens. But city leaders and workers were also activists and advocates for solving their cities' problems. Many saw different urban challenges—poverty, racism, environmental pollution, building deterioration and urban depopulation—as inextricably related and sought to solve them in tandem.[181]

In Cincinnati, this "active city" grew in the 1970s when a new left-leaning coalition took control of city council, ending decades of Republican-dominated politics. Comprising Democrats and Charterites (a liberal reform party originating in the 1920s), the coalition held a majority in city council from 1971 to 1985. As it was then custom for the mayor to be chosen from the majority party in council, the city's mayors in these years included Democrat Thomas Luken, Charterite Theodore Berry (Cincinnati's first African American mayor), Charterite Bobbie Sterne (Cincinnati's first full-term female mayor), Democrat James Luken and Democrat Jerry Springer. Democrats and Charterites asserted their commitment to community feedback and improving Cincinnati's quality of life. In this way, they showed themselves more invested in the lessons of liberal social activism of the 1960s and 1970s—movements like civil rights, environmentalism and feminism—than their Republican peers and predecessors.[182]

This new political culture encouraged the city's pursuit of a more equitable city, one that was more racially integrated, less physically deteriorated and more diverse across income. But city officials also wanted to devolve power to and listen to existing residents' visions for their neighborhoods. In Over-the-Rhine—like in many inner-city neighborhoods across the United States—these goals were often at odds, since existing residents in inner cities were wary of what capital reinvestment and higher incomes would do to the neighborhood. The result was continually evolving, often imperfect solutions by the city to its urban problems as it tried to accommodate its vision and that of existing residents.

In the 1960s, Cincinnati officials first used federal anti-poverty funds to remedy unsafe low-income housing in Over-the-Rhine. Around Findlay Market, it brought thousands of apartment units up to code, demolished about one thousand others and offered subsidies and technical assistance for the renovation of additional low-income housing. Federal assistance also went to new community organizations to coordinate anti-poverty social services for Over-the-Rhine.[183]

In 1966, the federal government's Model Cities program gave Cincinnati additional moneys to uplift its inner city. With these funds, the city's department of urban development (DUD) targeted Findlay Market, seeing it as a neighborhood cornerstone. The city thinking was that public investment there would help stimulate a larger revival throughout the neighborhood.

By the 1960s, the markethouse's columns and frame were rusting, and its structure failed to meet city building code. Model Cities money and local funds resolved these problems and also paid for updated electrical wiring, new incandescent lighting fixtures and tile flooring. Curb posts with electric outlets were additionally installed for outside vendors. Inside, the city put in heating and air conditioning. (Prior to this, temperatures on a summer day easily reached more than one hundred degrees, and in the winter it was cold inside.) The markethouse also received modern plumbing so that stalls had access to running water for the first time in the market's history. With these renovations, Elder Street on the north and south side of the markethouse became pedestrian only, helping to make the market more walkable and friendly to shoppers.[184]

The city also used Model Cities funds to pay for an Over-the-Rhine community center, which it built just to the southeast of Findlay Market (on top of several historic buildings, including St. John's Catholic Church). For that project, DUD listened to and collaborated with local neighborhood leaders who had a vision for a one-stop center for anti-poverty resources. The center—the Pilot Center, now the Over-the-Rhine Community Center—included employment services, housing resources, family counseling, nutrition aid, a center for neighborhood seniors, a health clinic and a general education development (GED) program. Work on the markethouse and community center was complete by June 1974.[185]

The Over-the-Rhine community welcomed the markethouse renovation and the Pilot Center. "To most people of Greater Cincinnati, the City Department of Urban Development is just another department of bureaucracy, a cold, impersonal part of the establishment. But to the Findlay Market people, the Department of Urban Development is a group of warm, friendly team-mates," wrote the Friends of Findlay Market, a volunteer group of local residents dedicated to serving the market. Similarly, many merchants at Findlay appreciated the city's renovation, although some felt like it was a long time coming. The impression remained among some business owners that the city was letting the market die—that as suburban grocery chains pulled customers away from Findlay Market, the city was not addressing the high vacancy and crime rate in Over-the-Rhine to get those customers back. This sentiment created antagonism between some vendors and the city, especially as the city raised rents post-renovation to cover market operating expenses.[186]

The markethouse prior to the 1970s renovation. *Courtesy of Archives and Rare Books, University of Cincinnati Libraries.*

Community planning session for the 1970s renovation of Findlay Market. *Courtesy of Archives and Rare Books, University of Cincinnati Libraries.*

Some of the Department of Urban Development (DUD) employees who worked with the community on the Findlay Market renovation. *Pictured at the markethouse, from left to right*: Ron Kull, Bob Rosen, Ned Callahan and Barry Cholak. For DUD's work at Findlay Market, the organization Friends of Findlay Market said that Kull and his colleagues were a group of "grass-rootsy resident dreamers and department people and architect designers." Friends of Findlay Market further said, "Nobody in Findlay Market will ever again think of agencies of the 'establishment' as cold bureaucracy." *Courtesy of Archives and Rare Books, University of Cincinnati Libraries.*

Meanwhile, Over-the-Rhine community organizers—while appreciative of the Pilot Center—remained concerned about the city's larger mission to redevelop the neighborhood into a mixed-income one, fearing historic preservation and economic development would push out existing low-income residents. In particular, many members of the Over-the-Rhine Community Council were worried, including Stanley "Buddy" Gray, a neighborhood resident and tireless advocate for Over-the-Rhine's homeless population. Gray and other affordable housing advocates defended Over-the-Rhine as it was, low-income and predominantly African American.[187]

Inspired by places like Harlem, New York City—a Black-majority neighborhood that thrived during its heydey in the 1920s—Gray and his allies felt that Over-the-Rhine as an African American community did not need economic development to feel empowered. And for sure, there was an important network of families and friends in Over-the-Rhine when Gray

This page: The groundbreaking for the 1970s renovation at Findlay Market. *Courtesy of Archives and Rare Books, University of Cincinnati Libraries.*

moved there in the 1970s. But there is a difference between Harlem in the 1920s—then dense and full of Black-owned businesses and Black-run social services—and Harlem in the 1970s, when it saw significant Black population loss, unemployment and deteriorated housing. Gray and his allies did not see this distinction. Nonetheless, as key community organizers in Over-the-Rhine, they were influential in their ideas since federal aid programs in the 1960s stipulated maximum participation from community members. Cities had to listen to everyday residents like Gray.[188]

This conflict—over remaking the downtown into a mixed-income area—came to a head when a coalition of historic preservationists, Over-the-Rhine residents, local businesses and city officials in DUD decided to make Over-the-Rhine a national historic district. The group submitted a nomination for historic district designation to the state and federal government in 1982. In 1972, Findlay Market was put in the National Register of Historic Places, and two years later, with support of several market merchants, the city zoned the area around it to prevent widespread demolition. But federal historic designation of the entire Over-the-Rhine neighborhood offered federal subsidies to renovate historic buildings there. Community activists, low-income housing advocates (including Gray) and even some city officials opposed the nomination, fearing that such incentives would cause significant displacement through extensive redevelopment. They were unsuccessful. The federal government approved the nomination in 1983. The designation coincided with the creation of Cincinnati's Historic Conservation Board (HCB) in 1980, tasked with creating conservation legislation and local historic districts and reviewing aspects of historic building renovations.[189]

While low-income housing advocates felt that they lost an important battle, they won another. The 1985 Over-the-Rhine Master Plan, created by community members like Gray, called for the vast majority of Over-the-Rhine's housing—at least 5,520 units—to be low-income. (For reference, there were 7,405 existing housing units in Over-the-Rhine in 1984.) Committed to letting a neighborhood speak for itself, the city approved this version of the master plan, agreeing that Over-the-Rhine could remain a predominantly low-income place. That said, the plan called for the area around Findlay Market to be revitalized as a commercial district. It also reiterated the city's goal to rehab at least 2,000 vacant units in the neighborhood, putting them back into productive use.[190]

City efforts around Findlay in the 1960s and 1970s preserved the markethouse and built an important community center, but over the next years, Over-the-Rhine continued to lose more population. It went from

This page and opposite: The markethouse stripped for renovation and signage for the work. The north side of the market square, clearly under construction. *Courtesy of Archives and Rare Books, University of Cincinnati Libraries.*

12,355 in 1980 to 9,572 in 1990. Poverty grew in this time, and near Findlay Market, a quarter of the buildings were vacant, reflective of the neighborhood's overall vacancy rate.[191]

To some stakeholders—city officials, Findlay Market businesses and a portion of Over-the-Rhine residents—this ongoing trend justified continuing and additional public and private reinvestment in the urban core to make it more mixed-income and less vacant. They felt that low-income housing developers like Thomas Denhart were holding the neighborhood back by making too much of Over-the-Rhine subsidized. Some leveled the same criticism at Buddy Gray, who in 1995 was the second-largest holder of property after Denhart, owning seventy-nine properties in the neighborhood, twenty-seven of them vacant.[192]

When we look at the results of anti-poverty efforts in cities in the 1960s, neighborhoods like Over-the-Rhine—where poverty only grew in the following years—suggest that the War on Poverty failed. That assessment fails to appreciate that so much was stacked against cities

This page and opposite: The markethouse's new interior and exterior, post-renovation. *Courtesy of Archives and Rare Books, University of Cincinnati Libraries, and Cincinnati Preservation Association.*

Above: The site for the new Pilot Center, on Elder Street east of the market. While the new center required the demolition of historic buildings, it created an important social services hub for Over-the-Rhine. *Courtesy of Archives and Rare Books, University of Cincinnati Libraries.*

Right: St. John's Church at Green and Republic Streets—which Christian Weber, the early shoemaker at Findlay Market, at least partially financed—was demolished for the new Pilot Center. The church tower, seen in the far right, was retained. *Courtesy of Archives and Rare Books, University of Cincinnati Libraries.*

succeeding in the first place. For one, loss of tax revenue through ongoing urban depopulation continued to drain city resources. National politics and the economy also played a role in preventing the success of anti-poverty work in cities. While the federal government had been providing cities with urban renewal funds since 1949, the Nixon administration in the 1970s reversed this, sending federal funds to suburbs and to new cities in the southwest Sunbelt area. The economic downturn of the 1970s—when Americans experienced declining real wages, growing

This page: New HUB center on Elder Street, just east of the market. *Courtesy of Archives and Rare Books, University of Cincinnati Libraries.*

This page and opposite: Scenes of building deterioration and vacancy around Over-the-Rhine, within three blocks of Findlay Market. Importantly, the neighborhood was never devoid of families, friends and community, even when one-fourth of its buildings sat empty. Still, Over-the-Rhine's level of poverty and disinvestment—due to white flight and institutional racism—was astonishing. *Author's collection.*

New senior services center on Race Street, just southeast of the market. *Courtesy of Archives and Rare Books, University of Cincinnati Libraries.*

unemployment, high inflation and manufacturing and industrial job loss due to automation and outsourcing—spelled the end of the post–World War II industrial boom. The poor economy compounded poverty already affecting inner-city communities. In the 1980s, the Reagan administration continued to cut federal funds to antipoverty and social welfare programs, further contributing to inner-city poverty. Under Reagan, private-sector solutions were instead stressed. This included getting private community development corporations (CDCs) to spearhead urban development.

In Over-the-Rhine, the war on poverty was further challenged by community members like Gray (who, we should mention, was tragically shot in 1996 by a mentally ill friend). Gray and his fellow activists appreciated the neighborhood for what it was, not what it could become. This perspective—that a war on poverty was unnecessary—complicated what the city could or should do for the Findlay Market area and the larger downtown core.

THE INVOLVED CITY:
ECONOMIC AND COMMUNITY DEVELOPMENT AT THE TURN OF THE TWENTY-FIRST CENTURY

Despite the downtown basin's enduring poverty and diminished federal aid, the city remained committed to its vision of a revived, racially integrated, mixed-income city center. Since federal funds for urban redevelopment dried up beginning in the 1970s—and as city tax revenue was tight with ongoing urban depopulation—city leaders in Cincinnati and in other U.S. cities pursued a new path to urban revival. They began to pair public investment with tax incentives, subsidies and grants for private developers as a way to draw investment back to the urban core. For instance, after the 1977 Community Reinvestment Act, Cincinnati began to offer temporary tax abatements for homeowners and developers in places like Over-the-Rhine where buildings—then at historically low property values—would see a dramatic rise in value and property tax with reinvestment. The city hoped that by offsetting a large tax bill, it would incentivize the private development it needed to revive its core. These kinds of public-private partnerships began to remake downtown Cincinnati in the 1980s, 1990s and early 2000s. Redevelopment started at the riverfront and worked its way north, getting to Findlay Market by the turn of the century.

Through these years, the city also remained committed to community empowerment and devolved decision-making. Democrats and Charterites continued to hold a majority on city council, and the city's mayors were all Democrats. They expressed their commitment to community development through a growing number of citywide initiatives. In 1981, the city used federal Community Development Block Grant funds to create a Neighborhood Support Program (NSP), a grant program for neighborhood improvement projects of people's own choosing. In 1989, the city used the same NSP program to establish annual stipends for community councils, funneling public money to neighborhood leaders. City officials also continued to care about existing low-income tenants, especially in Over-the-Rhine. Any time government money subsidized a real estate development project—renovating a dilapidated building or developing an underfunded area—the city mitigated displacement through federal or city relocation fees. The city's anti-displacement ordinance—crafted in 1980 and codified into the city charter—specifically provided assistance for displaced residences or businesses. Still, the city wrestled with affordability and inclusivity as it encouraged a mixed-income urban core.

It realized that while government-subsidized projects would make sure displaced persons had relocation assistance, private development projects would not necessarily do so. Furthermore, city officials confronted the fact that as they encouraged downtown reinvestment, rents would slowly rise across urban core neighborhoods, inadvertently causing removal with no resources for those affected.[193]

At the turn of the twenty-first century, each mayor and his or her administration confronted the issue of how to revive Cincinnati's center equitably and inclusively. Facing that quandary, each continued to pursue downtown redevelopment. Under Roxanne Qualls—mayor from 1993 to 1999—city council amended the 1985 Over-the-Rhine Master Plan to encourage the neighborhood's evolution into a mixed-income area, reversing its earlier approval of Over-the-Rhine as a predominantly low-income neighborhood. The plan targeted the southern half of the neighborhood for initial revitalization, establishing a low-interest loan pool of $9 million for development there. It also set aside $3 million of public and private money for Findlay Market. Encapsulating these actions, the city's 1994 Vision Task Force—an eleven-member team of community and business leaders—called for Over-the-Rhine's revitalization as a mixed-income neighborhood as the key to the entire city's success. While these plans laid the groundwork for reinvestment in Over-the-Rhine, little economic development occurred there in the 1980s and 1990s. A small trickle of private development occurred along Main Street south of Findlay Market, resulting in new bars, restaurants, art galleries and market-rate apartments there.[194]

Instead of Over-the-Rhine, city government under Qualls and her successor, Charlie Luken, first worked on the riverfront, believing that investment there would spur revitalization to the north, in Over-the-Rhine. A new master plan transformed the waterfront into a mixed-use area of market-rate housing, offices, restaurants, bars, hotels and ample parking, as well as the site of the National Underground Railroad Freedom Center, two new stadiums and a new riverfront park. The plan also laid the groundwork for a commuter light rail connecting northern Kentucky, Cincinnati's central business district, Over-the-Rhine and the University of Cincinnati, which manifested, years later in 2016, as the Cincinnati Bell Connector streetcar, running in a more limited loop from the river to Findlay Market. This downtown development in the early 2000s was yet another city effort to get residents, businesses and shoppers back to the basin. It did not all work according to plan. Paul Brown football stadium—

Cincinnati's remade riverfront, with Paul Brown Stadium on the left, Great American Ballpark on the right and the Banks mixed-use development in between. *Photo in the Carol M. Highsmith Archives, Library of Congress, Prints and Photographs Division.*

which Cincinnati taxpayers agreed to pay for through a 0.5 percent sales tax increase in return for a property tax rollback and additional public school funding—was massively over budget. Sales tax collections were half of what was expected from 1999 to 2008, indebting the county by millions and leading to a reverse of its property tax breaks. Given the economic recession in the early 2000s and the housing market crash in 2008, the stadiums made local government unpopular with many taxpayers.[195]

Luken, serving as mayor (for the second time) from 1999 to 2005, saw the stadium disaster unfold and the 2001 race riots, which left him only more determined to pursue urban revival—especially in Over-the-Rhine. Signaling the growing role of private, market-based solutions to urban problems, Luken's Economic Development Task Force recommended a private nonprofit corporation to spearhead downtown development. It would use public and private funding and work alongside the city and the Port Authority, Hamilton County's development agency. In 2003, the Cincinnati Center City Development Corporation (3CDC) was created for that purpose. It received initial funding from the Cincinnati Business Committee (CBC), a group organized in 1977 by sixteen executives from major Cincinnati-area businesses to assist the city with economic development. From there, 3CDC members—corporate executives like Procter & Gamble chief executive A.G. Lafley—created a private equity fund. To help, the city contributed millions of dollars in local tax incentives and offered access to federal community development grants. 3CDC used that aid, alongside New Market and other tax credits—incentives that reduce development entities' tax liability for their equity investments in historic and low-income development projects.[196]

In 2006, after 3CDC finished its renovation of Fountain Square in the central business district, it began its work in Over-the-Rhine. It purchased about one thousand parcels, including many former Section 8 buildings as well as corner liquor stores generating crime, which 3CDC closed down. It started its work on lower Vine Street, renovating buildings there into mixed-use, low-income and market-rate housing and commercial space. It next moved to Washington Park in the southern part of Over-the-Rhine—with a $47 million renovation—and then went north, toward Findlay Market.

Through the early 2000s, the city remained concerned about community involvement and inclusivity as the downtown underwent so many changes. Like it did for private development, it created a series of incentives and programs to fund neighborhood improvement and empowerment. In 2002, the city authorized Tax Incremental Financing (TIF) districts, where a portion of the tax revenue in neighborhoods seeing rising property values goes to a special fund for public improvements. With city approval, neighborhood community councils get to decide how to use the funding. In 2002, the city also set up its Notice of Funding Availability (NOFA) program, allocating gap financing to new housing projects through local and federal funds. NOFA awards prioritize projects that encourage homeownership or have a low-income rental component. In 2003, after complaints from business and neighborhoods leaders, city council streamlined city bureaucracy to make both economic and community development easier. The city merged the planning department with DED (the Department of Economic Development, the successor of DUD) and created a one-stop center for building permits. It also created more funding for neighborhood programs. In 2008, the city—then under the leadership of Mark Mallory, the city's first directly elected African American mayor—established the Neighborhood Enhancement Program (NEP). For that, the city selects a neighborhood for a ninety-day period of heightened city services like building code enforcement, beautification, crime prevention and city-resident engagement. In 2015, Over-the-Rhine was the recipient,

Washington Park sits to the immediate east of Cincinnati's iconic Music Hall. Here, 3CDC is in the midst of its renovation of the park. *Courtesy of 3CDC.*

with Grant Park—a park one block east of Findlay Market—the focus of the NEP funds.[197]

This litany of public efforts, beginning in the 1960s and growing over the subsequent years, shows the city's two-pronged approach to downtown revitalization: public-private economic development and neighborhood empowerment. Many city workers were well-meaning in their efforts to give agency to community organizations. Many cared about preventing displacement. But municipal revitalization work in the late twentieth century (through today) is not an unqualified success story, as it unfortunately left out many people. Residents rightfully remained concerned that the city was remaking the urban core into a place where they—as low-income individuals—would not belong. In Over-the-Rhine, people held strong opinions on this matter, dividing the neighborhood along lines of class, race and how long a person had lived there. For some African Americans there, the memory of urban renewal in the 1940s and 1950s—when large chunks of the downtown basin were demolished—convinced them that any public or private investment in poor neighborhoods was an effort to displace existing inhabitants. One African American woman who lived near Findlay Market commented in 1995, "Why would upper-class white people want to live in a ghetto? Without a doubt, they're doing all these repairs to move us out in the long run."[198]

THE INVOLVED CITY: FINDLAY MARKET UNDERGOES ANOTHER RENOVATION

While major renovation work in Over-the-Rhine and especially up by Findlay Market did not start until the early 2000s, the groundwork for another market renovation was laid in 1995 with the city's Findlay Market Master Development Plan. The city largely followed it, investing significant public and private funds into the market and the surrounding area in the early 2000s. As a part of this, it also bought, stabilized and sold numerous vacant buildings around the market square to private developers, hoping to spur economic development at Findlay. Nearby, in the northern part of Over-the-Rhine, the city worked with 3CDC and other private developers to redevelop abandoned buildings back into residential and commercial use. Through these efforts, the city tried to walk a fine line between encouraging widespread change and making sure that existing residents felt at home. In 1996, city council stated as much, saying, "Findlay Market should be developed as a regional marketplace and tourist attraction while respecting the tradition of serving local residents." Even with this intention, not all community members were pleased. As had been the case since the 1960s and 1970s, the city's dual interest in economic development and community empowerment remained difficult to coordinate.[199]

Findlay Market's 1995 master plan evolved from work in the late 1980s and early 1990s when the city again reimagined how much Findlay Market could serve as a cornerstone for downtown revitalization. This idea was inspired by successful public market revivals in Columbus, Chicago, Seattle and other cities. Seattle's Pike Place Market, which was established in 1907 as a farmers' market, had deteriorated by the 1960s to the point of facing demolition. Instead of razing it, the city saved it. In 1971, voters approved the area as a historic district, enabling the city to rehabilitate the markethouse buildings. By the early 1980s, it was seeing up to forty thousand visitors per day shopping across 230 diverse businesses. The City of Cincinnati hoped for a similar outcome at Findlay Market.[200]

To accomplish this, something needed to be done about the growing vacancy and physical deterioration on the market square, as merchants expressed to city officials. In 1993, Jean Bender of Bender Meats (and the leader of the Findlay Market Association) explained that crime had gotten so bad around Findlay Market that many merchants contemplated moving somewhere else. "How much does the historical value mean if you can't make people feel safe to be here?" she asked. Her concern did not fall on deaf ears. Mayor Qualls said at the time, "We can't allow Findlay Market to die just by neglect." By its own 1984 market study, the city tallied that 67 percent of the buildings on the market needed rehabilitation. But Qualls was also aware that significant public and private money would be needed for market renovations. At that time, the city made no profit from Findlay Market since subsidized rents there covered the market's utilities and just one city employee's salary.[201]

The 1995 master plan enabled the city to procure significant funding from federal, state and county sources that, along with privately fundraised dollars and city reserves, enabled major work on the market square. The plan grew from extensive consumer and neighborhood research, including what other markethouses were doing, and came about through the guidance of a steering committee of community stakeholders, including market merchants, neighborhood representatives, local civil rights leaders, property developers, police officers and city employees. The objective was to increase patronage at the market, have more diversity in merchandise, promote

This page and opposite: Findlay Market in the 1990s prior to its next big renovation. The market, despite its growing vacancy and deterioration, continued to draw diverse crowds from both city-center neighborhoods and from farther-out areas. *Courtesy of Archives and Rare Books, University of Cincinnati Libraries.*

small and minority-owned businesses and "maximize use of private investment in the development of the Findlay Market Business District." To accomplish these goals, plans included enlarging the markethouse, adding parking and building an outdoor farmers' market; the city would also obtain and stabilize a number of vacant buildings rimming the market. The master plan also suggested that the market connect minority businesses with city, state and federal business loans, and it called for the city to set up some kind of business incubator program to help entrepreneurs of color and lower economic means. The city followed this outline. With respect to the markethouse and square, renovation work—originally estimated to be $10 million—grew more costly as time went on and was slower than the city wanted. Major work on the markethouse was finished by 2004.[202]

From 2002 to 2004, the markethouse, stripped to its original cast- and wrought-iron frame, underwent renovation. It was enlarged from seven thousand to twelve thousand square feet. Operable full-lite garage-style doors were installed on the outside to protect exterior vendors from weather, and additional windows were added to the markethouse to brighten its interior. Mechanical systems in the markethouse were also updated. Even though heating and air conditioning were added in the 1974 renovation, the markethouse remained too hot in the summer, a major issue for vendors since the majority sold perishable meat, poultry and cheese. One, James L. Mackie of Mackie Meats, wrote to city council in 1985, begging them to install better mechanicals. "I am a long standing tenant with the city, having been there since before the market was renovated in 1974. Since that time I can only think of a few weeks when the cooling and heating system has functioned properly." He noted the problems that summer heat—ninety-five degrees inside the markethouse, he said—caused for his food quality.[203]

As part of its renovation, the city added an outdoor farmers' market to the north of the markethouse and constructed a parking lot to the north of that. The new parking required that an existing park and playfield be moved slightly to the east of Findlay Market along Vine Street. Since parking had emerged as a major sticking issue between merchants and the city by the 1980s—with businesses expressing that much more was needed in the area to keep Findlay Market attractive to a range of customers—the city decided it was imperative to move the playfield. That decision displeased some community members. When market manager Tom Jackson met with the city's park board, recreation commission and community organizations over the matter, the Over-the-Rhine Community Council and the Greater

The parking lot north of the market. *Courtesy of Archives and Rare Books, University of Cincinnati Libraries.*

Cincinnati Coalition for the Homeless protested, arguing that it would be unsafe for children to play so close to Vine Street, a busy thoroughfare. Furthermore, they said that the entire master plan for Findlay Market lacked community representation. In this point, plans for Findlay Market continued to show divisions in the neighborhood over race and class. It revealed the belief among some that city officials were not being as inclusive as they should be; this was especially held by community council leaders, who remained very protective of the point of view of low-income African American residents. The city, with park board and recreation commission support, moved forward with the plans for the playfield and parking lot. To Over-the-Rhine's community council, this was evidence that the city did not care about community wishes. To Findlay Market merchants, this was evidence that the city did care about the community since merchants—who were also a part of Over-the-Rhine—very much wanted parking. It was another moment when the city could not win, when its interest in economic development and community empowerment were at odds.[204]

Aside from the markethouse, the city's DED targeted the market square. One-fourth of the storefronts sat vacant, and as of 2000, only eight people—across thirty-three buildings—lived above the market square. For those few occupied units, the city made clear that "there should be no net loss of low income housing." For the rest, the city wanted to see "commercial at ground level with residential/housing uses on upper floors" that would be largely mixed-income.[205]

To facilitate this transformation, the city acquired multiple vacant buildings on the square—at 109, 111–113, 115, 112–120 and 129–133 West Elder—along with several properties to the east and west of the market. After stabilizing them, the city slowly sold them to private developers (a process that continues today), who were to "bring the buildings into use consistent with the recommendations of the Findlay Market Master Business Development Plan." In 2001, DED director Evonne L. Kovach reiterated the city's desire for these buildings, saying, "Structures with potential residential use will be maintained for redevelopment into safe and affordable housing....Following acquisition, the properties will be sold to developers or non-profits with the requirement that they be rehabilitated for mixed use/residential use."[206]

For a few city-owned properties at Findlay Market—112–116 West Elder and 118–120 West Elder on the north side—the city did additional work beyond stabilization prior to offloading them. As the markethouse was being upgraded, the businesses inside were temporarily displaced, so city officials renovated 112–120 West Elder's storefronts to provisionally house markethouse merchants. For that, the city totally revamped the first floors of these properties, removing all historic fabric, including the stairs to get to upper floors. This not only freed up square footage for the storefront tenants but also was seen as a money-saver by the city. By mothballing upper floors, the city could concentrate its resources on storefront renovations. This contradicted the city's stated goal to remake Findlay Market into "commercial at ground level with residential/housing uses on upper floors" but also illuminates the city's thinking around 2000. It *hoped* that in the future people would want to live in apartments above the market square. To this end, after it removed the stairs, the city had architectural plans drawn up for these buildings that showed future framing required for upper-floor accessibility. But around 2000, that rental interest did not yet exist; it would take another ten to twenty years to substantially develop. So, the stair removal made sense at that time. After all, the upper floors of 112–116 West Elder had been vacant since the late 1980s, the upper levels at 118 West Elder since 1995 and 120 West Elder's since the late 1960s.[207]

While the city's removal of historic stairs seems counter to its goal of historic preservation, in many other instances the city chose to save its old buildings and their historic parts. When the city acquired Findlay Market properties

This page: The North Addition buildings at 112–116 West Elder (on the right side of the upper image and the left side of the lower image) and 118–120 West Elder (the lighter building) under construction. *Courtesy of Archives and Rare Books, University of Cincinnati Libraries.*

around 2000, some of them were extensively fire damaged, and the city's own master plan suggested demolition on the market square. But DED and the department of buildings and inspections ultimately kept demolition to a bare minimum at the market, reflective of city officials' ongoing belief that historic preservation could reattract residents and businesses to Over-the-Rhine. In 2003, when the owner of 100 West Elder—the large building at the northeast corner of the market—took out a load-bearing wall, the back of the structure collapsed. Councilmember Jim Tarbell stepped in, fundraising $40,000 for its repair. City council then appropriated $250,000 to restore the back wall. Two years earlier, Tarbell got council to save and stabilize the front façade of 1721–1725 Vine Street, located just east of the market. The building had suffered a catastrophic fire, necessitating the department of buildings and inspections to raze the majority of it, but Tarbell insisted that the façade be saved, "incorporated into a new development."[208]

This city preservation work on the market square mirrors how, since around 2000, the city has procured vacant property from delinquent landlords

Left: The devastated state of 112–116 West Elder on the second floor, looking east. When the city acquired the buildings, upper floors had been vacant for years. *Courtesy of Archives and Rare Books, University of Cincinnati Libraries.*

Right: Inside the second floor of 114 West Elder. Due to neglect and abandonement, there were no wood floors, interior walls to demarcate rooms, fireplace mantels, ceilings or windows. Plaster walls were in a ruinous state. *Photo by author.*

Left: The city, in an effort to mothball deteriorated upper floors at 112–116 West Elder and concentrate on its storefront, removed the interior stairs to upper floors. The only way to the second floor was by a ladder cut through a hole in the plywood subflooring. *Photo by author.*

Right: Inside 112–114 West Elder, showing the cavity where the city removed the stairs leading from the second floor to the third. *Photo by author.*

throughout Over-the-Rhine. In an effort to prevent their demolition, it stabilizes the buildings and sells them to private developers. In some cases, the city recovers buildings that it previously had sold to developers who failed to take care of them. As a result of this, as time progressed, the city has become more rigorous in underwriting who it sells property to, making sure the entity is a capable developer. The city issues a public Request for Proposal (RFP); interested developers must not only prove their financial ability to renovate the city-owned building but must also go in front of the neighborhood's community council and city council, seeking those bodies' approval. The city has also acquired derelict building stock through foreclosures about to go to the sheriff auction, placing those properties in its "landbank program." Hamilton County, which encompasses the incorporated city, now runs the landbank program, selling structures to well-intentioned owners at slightly under market value.[209]

While the city's process of stabilizing and selling city-owned properties throughout Over-the-Rhine continues today, its renovation of the markethouse was complete by 2004. Work was held up by the April 2001 racial unrest in Over-the-Rhine. Protests turned violent and damaged the storefronts at 112–120 West Elder—just before the displaced markethouse vendors moved into them—forcing the city to spend an additional $175,000. Across the market, several storefronts were vandalized, including Heist's Fish and Poultry and Leader Furniture, which like other buildings nearby saw their front windows smashed. The main house was unscathed fortunately. Following the riots, many market merchants reported significantly smaller sales, leading the city to waiving and lowering rent rates for different vendors. That said, on the first Saturday that the market was open after the riots, merchants reported crowds twice the usual size, with many customers saying they came to Findlay Market to show their support. Mayor Luken, in attendance, stated, "This is the cornerstone of development in Over-the-Rhine, and it needs support."[210]

As part of its twenty-first-century market renovation and evidence of its belief in public-private partnerships, the city created a private, nonprofit organizational entity to manage Findlay Market once the construction work was complete. In 2004, while retaining ownership of Findlay's businesses, the city transferred the management and development of the market to the Corporation for Findlay Market (CFFM), with Robert J. Pickford as its first executive director. This move followed similar actions by other cities. Columbus's North Market established a development nonprofit to relay between merchants and City of Columbus officials, and Seattle's Pike Place also had a development authority managing the market.[211]

At its creation, CFFM's mission was to continue the market's development into a thriving and growing public market "that spurs economic development in the surrounding neighborhood." The market, as expressed by Pickford, should serve the immediate neighborhood but also the metropolitan whole; it should attract people at all times of the day as a center for small food-centered retail; it should be fully leased; and it should be located in "a safe, walkable Over-the-Rhine neighborhood that enjoys a growing residential population." Such objectives placed CFFM in the same line of thought as city officials—that Over-the-Rhine could and should be home to a diversity of businesses and a variety of people, including low-income ones.[212]

A key goal of the city's market renovation—and its downtown development in general—was to diversify business opportunities at Findlay Market and throughout Over-the-Rhine. The Findlay Market master plan stated as much, saying, "In recognition of the fact that a disproportionate number of African Americans are customers in the current mix, there should be more vendors and employees who are African American, especially neighborhood residents." To achieve this, the city used federal money to create a loan program to aid minority entrepreneurs who wanted to establish a business. It also created and allocated $100,000 for a kitchen incubator to provide training and offer subsidized business space for different kinds of entrepreneurs, including women and persons of color.[213]

Soon after its establishment, CFFM entered into an agreement with the Greater Cincinnati/Northern Kentucky African American Chamber of Commerce (AACC) to recruit minority lease applicants for Findlay Market stalls. Within a year of CFFM's management, Findlay Market welcomed five new minority vendors: three women, one white, one from the Philippines and one African American; an African American male proprietor; and another business owned by a first-generation immigrant from the Middle East. In 2005, the city also dedicated additional moneys to the MicroCity Loan Fund operated by the Greater Cincinnati Microenterprise Initiative, which worked with the CFFM to recruit minority merchants.[214]

In 2014, after many years of planning, CFFM launched its Findlay Kitchen, a shared kitchen space that provides affordable access to commercial-grade kitchen equipment and storage space, located just to west of the market. As of 2020, 80 percent of Findlay Kitchen members were immigrants, women and other individuals of a minority background. In 2018, as a part of Findlay Kitchen, the city extended a loan to CFFM for a storefront accelerator program. In storefronts to the immediate west of the market, Findlay Kitchen graduates and other new food entrepreneurs have been given space to test their concept for short nine-month tenures at subsidized rents. The goal is to mentor woman-, immigrant- and minority-owned food businesses so that they can move to more permanent locations in Cincinnati. This happened for Isis Arrieta-Dennis, a Colombian immigrant, who started Arepa Place—a Colombian-Venezuelan restaurant—in Findlay Kitchen and moved to a storefront right on the market in 2018. Similarly, Sarah Dworak, a Ukrainian-American, and her business partner, Iwona Przybysz, a first-generation Polish immigrant, started Babushka Pierogies in 2012, went through the Findlay Kitchen program and then moved to a storefront on Main Street in Over-the-Rhine where they sell Polish-Ukrainian fare.[215]

To make the market more accessible for low-income shoppers, CFFM expanded its food assistance program in 2007. Customers could then exchange their food assistance dollars—their Electronic Benefit Transfer (EBT) card dollars—for gold tokens to more easily shop around the market at a growing number of participating vendors. Furthermore, the Supplemental

This page and opposite: Findlay Market after its most recent renovation. It continues to operate as a neighborhood hub and tourist attraction, sitting in a neighborhood under construction. *Photos in the Carol M. Highsmith Archives, Library of Congress, Prints and Photographs Division.*

Nutrition Assistance Program (SNAP) matches each dollar (up to ten dollars) spent at the market, providing a limited but helpful dollar-for-dollar incentive to help low-income families have access to healthy, local food.[216]

The market improvements made by the city around 2000 brought changes for businesses there, with CFFM as their new landlord. The establishment of a nonprofit to manage the market—instead of the city—was recommended by multiple outside parties for efficiency's sake. Aside from that, the city created CFFM to have an intermediary between it and market merchants, thinking that a more hands-off relationship between the city and the market would foster more congeniality and cooperation between local government and Findlay businesses. While many community residents applauded the way that the city continued to care for the market, some businesses there were less pleased with the city, feeling that the renovations were too long in coming.

Still, post-renovation, most merchants cited an increase in customer traffic. Matt Madison of Madison's Grocery on the north side of the market called the city's renovation "an incredible stimulation." His next-door neighbor, Dean Zaidan of Dean's Mediterranean Imports, similarly said, "The renovation and changes have increased the volume of business from people who know about the market and what's available here. We also have people who are now coming to the market who have never been—and they've lived their whole life in Cincinnati." The updates at the markethouse encouraged more business; so did the renovation work around the square. As the city has slowly offloaded property there, developers have taken shell structures and turned them back into use, with commercial storefronts and upstairs residences. For a few buildings on the market square, the city retained ownership of the storefronts, working with CFFM to fill them with tenants; meanwhile, it sold the "air rights" to upper floors to private developers, who have turned the vacant spaces into apartments and condominiums. By 2017, most of the storefronts rimming the markethouse had commercial tenants once again.[217]

AN ONGOING PUBLIC-PRIVATE VENTURE AROUND THE MARKET

During and since the city's makeover of Findlay Market, private developers have renovated numerous buildings throughout the neighborhood. With 3CDC and the Model Group, another major developer, the city entered into preferred developer agreements, hastening Over-the-Rhine's physical transformation through public-private partnerships. In 2012, after 3CDC finished its renovation of Washington Park, it moved north to Findlay Market after entering into an agreement with the city to develop thirty-five city-owned parcels near the market. 3CDC renovated some buildings, while selling others to be rehabbed into residential and commercial properties, including affordable housing. In 2014, the city began to work with the Model Group, selling it numerous vacant buildings around Findlay Market, which Model has turned into mixed-use developments.[218]

All of this work has physically transformed Over-the-Rhine, including the Findlay Market area. Around 2000, one-fourth of the neighborhood's buildings were vacant. By 2015, the vast majority of housing units in the southern half of the neighborhood were occupied or occupiable with residents. By Findlay Market—indicative that renovation activity had been concentrated in the south of Over-the-Rhine—more than 40 percent of units still sat vacant, although that was slowly changing. Across the neighborhood, 82 percent of all units in 2015 were rentals in multi-unit buildings, indicative that the neighborhood remained a renter's market—and a low-income one to an extent. In 2015, around one-quarter of all Over-the-Rhine housing was for households truly considered low-income—those earning 30 percent or less of the area's AMI, which was then a little over $71,000. Of these, almost 40 percent were subsidized. Another 46 percent of units in the neighborhood in 2015 provided homes for those earning 30 to 60 percent of the AMI; and another 26 percent targeted those earning between 61 and 100 percent of the AMI. In the area around Findlay Market, 25 percent of the housing was truly low-income, and almost half of the rest supplied space for families earning between 30 and 60 percent of the area's AMI.[219]

This data suggests a mixed-income Over-the-Rhine, indicating that the city has been successful in its mission to introduce economic diversity to the neighborhood. But the introduction of higher incomes into the neighborhood has meant a loss of very low-income housing there. In 2016, a study was released that showed a 73 percent loss in housing for AMIs of 30 percent or less from 2002 to 2015—a loss of about 2,300 units. The study, funded by Over-the-Rhine Community Council and performed by Xavier University's Community Building Institute, surveyed current property owners and rent-listing websites and used data from the 2000 census to estimate earlier amounts of low-income housing. Some community stakeholders, many of them low-income housing advocates, view the study as evidence of ongoing displacement. Other community members disagree. They argue that the loss of low-income housing from 2002 to 2015 should not be solely blamed on

This page and opposite: Recent scenes from the Findlay Market area, especially Race Street to the east, showing a neighborhood under construction. *Author's collection.*

economic development since that would ignore how Thomas Denhart and other low-income housing developers offloaded thousands of Section 8 units in the neighborhood in the early 2000s, contributing to a significant loss in low-income housing. Furthermore, others in the neighborhood argue that since Over-the-Rhine had gotten so impoverished—to the point that 90 percent of occupied units were very low-income subsidized ones in 2002— then any subsequent economic development was going to reduce that very high percentage of low-income housing.[220]

These debates around development, affordability and inclusion in Over-the-Rhine continue with the release of the 2020 census. Despite the massive investment in the neighborhood, the census revealed that from 2010 to 2020, Over-the-Rhine's population dropped, decreasing from 6,062 to 5,622. Furthermore, according to the census, the neighborhood lost housing units. In 2010, there were around 4,300; ten years later, there were just over 3,800. Positively, more units were occupied in 2020 than in 2010—3,002 compared with 2,330. The decrease in vacancy signals ongoing renovation work in the neighborhood, and the loss of housing units could point to this construction work since there were buildings in 2010 that had people living in them that in 2020 were being renovated and brought up to building code.

However, the loss of units also suggests that as developers fix up buildings, some are constructing larger apartments, resulting in a net loss of units. While efforts to transform long-vacant buildings back into reuse is a positive thing for the neighborhood, the loss of density—in a neighborhood that bled population for the past several decades—is not good. Furthermore, developers' proclivity to create spacious units within newly renovated buildings means that they can charge more per square foot. They then price out many of the neighborhood's longtime residents and the many service-industry workers who work at Over-the-Rhine's growing number of bars, restaurants and shops. To this point, the census reported that over the past decade, Over-the-Rhine lost almost two thousand African American residents. In 2010, the neighborhood was 72 percent Black and 25 percent white; in 2020, it was 43 percent Black and 47 percent white. While this data shows a more racially integrated, mixed-income neighborhood—which on the surface sounds like a positive development—it has meant displacement of families of color.[221]

We know that race and class are intertwined in America due to our country's long history of racial and economic discrimination, and we know that communities of color have disproportionately had to live in divested urban core neighborhoods. Efforts to uplift these places for existing and new residents—which is a noble goal—expose how by making a place more income-diverse, the neighborhood becomes less racially diverse. What's happening in Over-the-Rhine begs the question confronting every U.S. city undergoing an urban revival right now. If we want truly diverse city centers, then how can government and private development renovate an urban core—which saw significant population loss and divestment over the twentieth century—without raising the costs of living there, given that existing residents are more likely to be persons of color and of lower economic means? Or, since rising costs of living are an inevitable consequence of urban reinvestment, how can government officials, developers and community leaders mitigate the effects for existing low-income residents? Or rather, instead of renovating a city *around* its low-income population, how do leaders *include* families on low and fixed incomes so that—for those interested in social mobility—wealth and business opportunities reach them as well? A neighborhood's transition from extreme poverty to income diversity does not have to mean displacement of existing residents, although it usually does.

Economic development officials in the city of Cincinnati, along with council members, have wrestled with these questions since the late twentieth century. In their solutions and actions—which many will disagree with and find inequitable—we nonetheless can appreciate that many city administrators and leaders saw themselves as advocates trying their best for their city centers. This attitude—wanting to remake urban cores into densely populated, vibrant places for many to live, work and spend time—shows a crucial shift in urban planning that began in the 1960s and continues to this day.

THE MARKET TODAY

F indlay Market today is indicative that people are caring about cities again. Since the city's last renovation of the market in the early 2000s, Findlay has seen a diversity of businesses begin, commercial vacancy decline and record numbers of people shopping there. Local families from the downtown basin go there, as do many suburban Cincinnatians and out-of-town visitors. Its popularity reflects Over-the-Rhine's as an increasingly popular place to shop, live and work. This slow reversal of white flight and urban divestment is occurring in many cities across the United States, where city centers are seeing people—professionals, young families, older retirees—returning to live, run a business or shop local. They join the people who never left, like many of Over-the-Rhine's African American families.

Findlay Market today retains qualities that helped it through the urban crisis of the twentieth century. It still has that old-world charm, with businesses that can trace their roots to early immigrants. It is still fairly affordable, with several merchants working with food assistance programs. It does offer boutique items, but most businesses cater to people's everyday grocery needs. It is still relevant. Shopping there, a person can almost get all the household supplies they need, although some basic items—things like toilet paper—are hard to come by. While many of the businesses are newer, established in the last five years, there are exceptions—places like Saigon Market and Dean's Mediterranean, which have been there since the 1970s, not to mention even older businesses. These mainstays make shoppers feel a deep connection to Findlay. But the newer businesses are proving important to customers too. Many are women- and minority-owned and offer locally made, zero-waste and organic products, signaling that the city and CFFM want these kinds of ventures at the market—and also that there is a consumer demand for them.

The city still owns the market, maintaining that almost 170-year relationship with Findlay. At the market and in the surrounding neighborhoods, it continues to embrace historic preservation as a key tool in rebuilding and repopulating the urban core into a mixed-income downtown, showing how far local government has come since its anti-dense planning of the mid-twentieth century. The city also continues to work with private entities to redevelop the downtown basin, perpetuating the public-private partnerships it began around 2000. Around Findlay Market, the city has especially worked with Model Group, which has renovated a significant number of vacant buildings nearby the market as part of a large "Market Square" development.

As city centers like Cincinnati's undergo so much change, Findlay Market's growing number of minority-owned businesses reminds us of the weight of the situation: that we must be remaking our urban core neighborhoods into diverse and inclusive spaces with a variety of residents and businesses. In Cincinnati, some local developers, including those working around Findlay, are sensitive to issues of equity and will partner with entities like Over-the-Rhine Community Housing to develop low-income housing. There are also local developers who renovate with density in mind, keeping units smaller to make them more affordable. Additionally, the city continues to encourage developers to turn rental properties into mixed-income apartments, doing so through competitive subsidies and incentives. In 2019, the city partnered with 3CDC and Model Group for a large twenty-building development project south of Findlay Market in Over-the-Rhine. Known as Willkommen ("Welcome"), the project will have a mixture of affordable and market-rate units, and for that, investors will receive a variety of tax credits.

Developments like Willkommen are market-driven solutions to problems of housing affordability. For low-income families, they provide accessibly priced, newly renovated housing. For families of higher AMIs, they provide essential neighborhood income diversity. For developers, the tax breaks that they receive for doing mixed-income projects take away some of the risk, making them able to keep investing in the neighborhood.

But the vision of Cincinnati's center as an income and racially diverse place remains elusive, and downtown Cincinnati has a long way to go before being an integrated community. There are many things that city leaders and community stakeholders need to do to address equity, but one key to having an integrated community is making sure that its members feel that they matter—that their voices are heard and respected. The city began to care about citizen participation in the 1960s, and while many municipal employees and elected officials still do, there are exceptions. Some public-private development deals for housing and other projects bulldoze over community concerns and input, rightfully earning local government and private corporations the reputation of being unaccountable and uninterested in democratic processes. That kind of political culture is toxic to a city and undermines all the great work that sensitive city officials and well-meaning private entities have done.

We do and must continue to pay attention to housing and how it will be priced. This is an incredibly important topic since it's one of the most basic human needs. And everyone deserves the right to affordable housing. City leaders and others in positions of power also need to continue to address why certain groups need housing assistance in the first place. When we think about that question, we're reminded of how racial discrimination has resulted in greater poverty for communities of color. As we as a nation wrestle with structural racism, Findlay Market's past reminds us of how unjust it was that African Americans—who were the majority of residents around the market for much of the twentieth century—were denied opportunities for social mobility there.

New people moving into revitalizing neighborhoods like Over-the-Rhine is not a bad thing. Instead, it should remind us of the continual evolution of our inner cities. With Over-the-Rhine, many groups moved into the neighborhood over the past two hundred years. Findlay Market was built and sustained by these waves of newcomers. Their presence—that ethnic, racial and socioeconomic diversity—is a major reason why people shopped and shop at Findlay. To me, as a shopper, it is one of the few truly diverse spots in Cincinnati.

However, as new people come into city centers and as economic development follows that growing demand, failing to diversify wealth there for those interested in social mobility is a great injustice. Business mentorship and incubator programs for entrepreneurs of color—like Findlay Kitchen—are a great start to expanding capital and opportunities for existing communities in inner cities. Federal, state and local government incentives and subsidies for minority-owned businesses, nonprofits and other ventures are similarly important. What else can we do in this important moment when so many cities are being remade?

NOTES

Introduction

1. In this book, "downtown" refers to the three oldest neighborhoods in its basin: the central business district by the riverfront, Over-the-Rhine to the north and the West End to the west.

Chapter 1

2. Roger Daniels, *Coming to America: A History of Immigration and Ethnicity in American Life*, 2nd ed. (New York: Harper Perennial, 1990, 2002), 148–50; Bruce Levine, *The Spirit of 1848: German Immigrants, Labor Conflict, and the Coming of the Civil War* (Urbana: University of Illinois Press, 1992), 15–34; Caroline Williams, *The City on Seven Hills* (Cincinnati, OH: Ruter Press, 1938), 58.
3. Joseph S. Stern Jr., "Findlay Market and Over-the-Rhine Revisited," *Cincinnati Historical Society Bulletin* 34, no. 1 (Spring 1976): 40, 43; Corporation for Findlay Market (hereafter CFFM), "A Brief History," https://www.findlaymarket.org/history.
4. "Cincinnati, City of Markets," *Cincinnati Enquirer*, September 15, 1929.
5. Stern, "Findlay Market and Over-the-Rhine Revisited," 30; CFFM, "Brief History"; Wendell Calhoun, Bureau of Agricultural Economics, United States Department of Agriculture, and Master Planning Division,

City Planning Commission of Cincinnati, *The Wholesale Fruit and Vegetable Market of Cincinnati: Present Operations and Future Needs* (Cincinnati, OH: City Planning Commission, 1946), 1.

6. James M. Mayo, *The American Grocery Store: The Business Evolution of an Architectural Space* (Westport, CT: Greenwood Press, 1993), 4–5, 11–17.

7. Ibid., 4–11.

8. Liz Tilton, *Cincinnati's Historic Findlay Market* (Charleston, SC: Arcadia Publishing, 2009), 18–19; Mayo, *American Grocery Store*, 18.

9. Williams' City Directories.

10. City Council, "A Ordinance—Markets: Defining the Spaces of and Regulating the Markets within the City of Cincinnati, and to Repeal Ordinances Therein Named," 1860–69, Cincinnati History Library and Archives, Cincinnati Museum Center (hereafter CMC), Cincinnati, Ohio; Helen Tangiers, *Movable Markets: Food Wholesaling in the Twentieth-Century City* (Baltimore, MD: Johns Hopkins University Press, 2019), 22–23.

11. City of Cincinnati City Council, "Report of the Special Committee of the City Council of Cincinnati on the Application of the Cincinnati & Indiana R.R. Co., For a Lease of the Pearl Street Market-Space," 1863, CMC.

12. "New Markethouses," *Cincinnati Enquirer*, August 2, 1881; "Cleansing the Markets," *Cincinnati Enquirer*, July 22, 1881.

13. Silas Chapman, *Chapman's Rail Road Map of Ohio, Indiana, Michigan, Illinois, Missouri, Minnesota, & Wisconsin*, map (Milwaukee, WI: S. Chapman, 1859), from the Library of Congress, Map Collections, https://www.loc.gov/resource/g4061p.rr001220/?r=0.11,0.392,1.78,0.767,0; Sherry O. Hessler, "'The Great Disturbing Cause' and the Decline of the Queen City," *Bulletin of the Historical and Philosophical Society of Ohio* 20, no. 3 (July 1962): 182.

14. Tangiers, *Movable Markets*, 74.

15. Daniels, *Coming to America*, 149–50; Clifford Neal Smith, *Early Nineteenth-Century German Settlers in Ohio (Mainly Cincinnati and Environs), Kentucky, and Other States, Parts 1, 2, and 3, and 4A: Surnames A through J, 4B: Surnames K through Z, 4C: Appendices* (McNeal, AZ: Westland Publications, 1984, 1988, 1991), 15.

16. Daniels, *Coming to America*, 145, 150.

17. Smith, *Early Nineteenth-Century German Settlers in Ohio*, 15.

18. Williams' City Directories; Find A Grave, "Stephen Spies," https://www.findagrave.com/memorial/99221596/stephen-spies.

19. Find A Grave, "Theodor Kunkel," https://www.findagrave.com/memorial/143081902/theodor-kunkel; Tilton, *Cincinnati's Historic Findlay*

Market, 10; death card for Theodore Kunkel, Cincinnati Birth and Death Records, 1865–1912, Digital Resource Commons (hereafter DRC), University of Cincinnati Libraries, Cincinnati, Ohio.

20. Williams' City Directories; Walnut Hills Historical Society, "Frederick Alms," http://www.walnuthillsstories.org/stories/frederick-alms; Find A Grave, "William Herman Alms," https://www.findagrave.com/memorial/38674239/william-herman-alms.

21. Author's interview with Vickie Hahn, April 27, 2021; Find A Grave, "Christian Weber," https://www.findagrave.com/memorial/79066593/christian-weber; 1870 Federal Census, ancestry.com; "Many Friends Pay Tribute to the Bier of Mrs. Rosa Weber," *Cincinnati Enquirer*, November 27, 1901; Williams' City Directories; "Store," *Cincinnati Enquirer*, January 19, 1892.

22. Williams' City Directories; 1870 Federal Census; Ohio, U.S., Wills and Probate Records, 1786–1998, ancestry.com.

23. "Sale of Money," *Cincinnati Enquirer*, January 2, 1887; "Building Associations," *Cincinnati Enquirer*, August 12, 1894.

24. Find A Grave, "Charles Kuchenbuch," https://www.findagrave.com/memorial/146607108/charles-j.-kuchenbuch; "Funeral Rites Tomorrow," *Cincinnati Enquirer*, February 10, 1928.

25. United States, Civil War Soldier Records and Profiles, 1861–65, ancestry.com; Gustav Tafel, *The Cincinnati Germans in the Civil War*, translated by Don Heinrich Tolzmann (Milford, OH: Little Miami Publishing Company, 2010), 15–16, 19; Levine, *Spirit of 1848*, 226; Carl Wittke, *Refugees of Revolution: The German Forty-Eighters in America* (Philadelphia: University of Pennsylvania Press, 1952), 18–28.

26. "Death of Nicholas Hoeffer," *Cincinnati Enquirer*, January 22, 1875; Find A Grave, "Nicholaus Diehl," https://www.findagrave.com/memorial/107151642/nicholaus-diehl; "Ohio, County Marriage Records, 1774–1993"; 1880, 1900 and 1910 Federal Censuses, ancestry.com; A.P. Sandles and E.W. Doty, *The Biographical Annals of Ohio, 1906–1907–1908: A Handbook of the Government and Institutions of the State of Ohio*, Ohio General Assembly, 1906–8, 427.

27. Victor Gross, *Cincinnati: The Queen City, 1788–1912* (Chicago: S.J. Clarke Publishing Company, 1912), retrieved from books.google.com.

28. "Grocers to Number of Nineteen Sued in Federal Court for Alleged Infringement of a Trademark—Serious Charges Preferred," *Cincinnati Enquirer*, September 3, 1899.

29. Mayo, *American Grocery Store*, 44.

30. Williams' City Directories; death card for August Siegmann, DRC; 1900 and 1910 Federal Censuses, ancestry.com; Michael Marks Davis, *Immigrant Health and the Community* (New York: Harper and Brothers Publishers, 1921), 184.
31. "An Extraordinary Story," *Cincinnati Enquirer*, March 4, 1874.
32. Williams' City Directories; 1900 and 1910 Federal Censuses, ancestry.com; birth card for John Sigmund, DRC.
33. 1860 Federal Census, ancestry.com; Williams' City Directories.
34. 1900 Federal Census, ancestry.com; death cards for Anna, Caroline, Elizabeth, Joseph, John and Frank Siegmann, DRC; Richard A. Meckel, *Save the Babies: American Public Health Reform and the Prevention of Infant Mortality, 1850–1929* (Baltimore, MD: Johns Hopkins University Press, 1990), 1.
35. "In the Dark," *Cincinnati Enquirer*, November 11, 1888.
36. "The Cowardly Crime of a Father," *Cincinnati Enquirer*, January 13, 1883.
37. "Death of Robert Hoffman," *Cincinnati Enquirer*, February 26, 1883.
38. Stephen Z. Starr, "Prosit!!!!: A Non-Cosmic Tour of the Cincinnati Saloon," *Cincinnati Historical Society Bulletin* 36, no. 3 (Fall 1978): 176.

Chapter 2

39. "Findlay Market," *Cincinnati Enquirer*, December 21, 1902.
40. George M. Henzel, "Over-the-Rhine—USA," *Cincinnati Historical Society Bulletin* 40, no. 1 (Spring 1982): 7.
41. Zane L. Miller and Bruce Tucker, *Changing Plans for America's Inner Cities: Cincinnati's Over-the-Rhine and Twentieth-Century Urbanism* (Columbus: Ohio State University Press, 1998), xix.
42. Alan M. Kraut, "Silent Travelers: Germs, Genes, and American Efficiency, 1880–1924," *Social Science History* 12, no. 4 (Winter 1988): 377–78; *1912 Report on the Survey of the Foreign Population in Cincinnati*, Public Library of Cincinnati and Hamilton County.
43. Starr, "Prosit," 177.
44. Williams' City Directories; 1900 Federal Census, ancestry.com; Starr, "Prosit," 181.
45. 1900 Federal Census, ancestry.com; "Vigorous Prosecution," *Cincinnati Enquirer*, November 18, 1902; "Damages for Injury," *Cincinnati Enquirer*, January 12, 1906; "Circuit Court Says No," *Cincinnati Enquirer*, March 9, 1907; Williams' City Directories; Find A Grave, "Ludwig Seegmueller," https://

www.findagrave.com/memorial/173202721/ludwig-seegmüller; Starr, "Prosit," 177, 185.

46. Starr, "Prosit," 186.
47. 1900 and 1910 Federal Censuses, ancestry.com; "No Fancy Dishes at Banquet of Cin'ti Cooks," *Cincinnati Post,* January 3, 1908; Starr, "Prosit," 184.
48. Williams' City Directories.
49. Interview with Jim Kennedy, April 29, 2021, and May 21, 2021; Find A Grave, "Christian Sachs," https://www.findagrave.com/memorial/29095580/christian-sachs; Hamburg Passenger Lists, 1850–1934; Ohio, U.S., County Marriage Records, 1774–1993, ancestry.com; Find A Grave, "William J. Sachs Sr.," https://www.findagrave.com/memorial/29095682/william-j-sachs.
50. Williams' City Directories; "To Enlarge," *Cincinnati Enquirer*, January 31, 1912; "Sachs Will Be Named Mayor on German Day," *Cincinnati Post*, August 3, 1937; "Christian Sachs," *Cincinnati Enquirer*, December 31, 1938.
51. Zane L. Miller, "Cincinnati Germans and the Invention of an Ethnic Group," *Queen City Heritage* 42, no. 3 (Fall 1984): 13.
52. Williams' City Directories.
53. Ann Deborah Michael, "The Origins of the Jewish Community of Cincinnati, 1817–1860," *Cincinnati Historical Society Bulletin* 30, no. 3–4 (Fall/Winter 1972): 155.
54. Daniels, *Coming to America*, 223–24; Zane L. Miller, *Boss Cox's Cincinnati: Urban Politics in the Progressive Era* (Columbus: Ohio State University Press, 1968, 2000), 13.
55. 1920 Federal Census, ancestry.com; Find A Grave, "Gus Loewenstein Jr.," https://www.findagrave.com/memorial/141640631/gus-loewenstein; "Social Affairs," *Cincinnati Enquirer*, April 30, 1901.
56. Michael, "Origins of the Jewish Community of Cincinnati," 180; Miller, *Boss Cox's Cincinnati*, 130, 175.
57. "Butchers and Butchering," *Cincinnati Enquirer*, October 12, 1884; "Mayor's Choice," *Cincinnati Enquirer*, April 11, 1886; "A Swift Session," *Cincinnati Enquirer*, August 25, 1887; "Gus' Pudding," *Cincinnati Enquirer*, September 23, 1886; "Ten-Thousand-Dollar Snap," *Cincinnati Enquirer*, August 28, 1886.
58. David Stradling, *Cincinnati: From River City to Highway Metropolis* (Charleston, SC: Arcadia Publishing, 2003), 78–79.
59. Stern, "Findlay Market and Over-the-Rhine Revisited," 43.

60. "Popcorn and Shoe Strings the Foundation of a Fortune," *Cincinnati Enquirer*, April 23, 1912; Michael, "Origins of the Jewish Community of Cincinnati," 175.

61. "Popcorn and Shoe Strings."

62. "Royal," *Cincinnati Enquirer*, November 16, 1901; "Gorgeous Affair at Goldsmith's," *Cincinnati Enquirer*, March 22, 1903; "Powerful," *Cincinnati Enquirer*, November 20, 1902.

63. Find A Grave, "Jacob Friedman," https://www.findagrave.com/memorial/185980188/jacob-friedman; 1900, 1910 and 1920 Federal Censuses, ancestry.com; Ownership Card, Hamilton County Auditor.

64. Michael, "Origins of the Jewish Community of Cincinnati," 178; Williams' City Directories; 1910, 1920 and 1940 Federal Censuses, ancestry.com; Find A Grave, "Morris Loshinsky," https://www.findagrave.com/memorial/139735587/morris-loshinsky.

65. Barbara L. Musselman, "The Shackles of Class and Gender: Cincinnati Working Women, 1890–1920," *Queen City Heritage* 41, no. 4 (Winter 1983): 37.

66. Nancy E. Bertaux, "'Women's Work' vs. 'Men's Work' in Nineteenth Century Cincinnati," *Queen City Heritage* 47, no. 4 (Winter 1989): 18.

67. Annette Mann, *Women Workers in Factories* (Cincinnati, OH: Consumers' League of Cincinnati, 1918), 43.

68. "Seamstresses," *Cincinnati Enquirer*, April 11, 1881; "Finishers," *Cincinnati Enquirer*, June 30, 1889; "Young Lady," *Cincinnati Post*, October 12, 1922; 1900, 1910 and 1920 Federal Censuses, ancestry.com; Williams' City Directories.

69. Mann, *Women Workers in Factories*, 35–36.

70. 1900, 1910 and 1920 Federal Censuses, ancestry.com; Musselman, "Shackles of Class and Gender," 38.

71. Mann, *Women Workers in Factories*, 38.

72. 1920 and 1930 Federal Censuses, ancestry.com; Williams' City Directories.

73. 1900 and 1910 Federal Censuses, ancestry.com; Find A Grave, "Sophia Siehl," https://www.findagrave.com/memorial/144518378/sophia-siehl, and "Amelia Peal," https://www.findagrave.com/memorial/79012308/amelia-c.-peal.

74. Author's interview with Tom Wegner, May 15, 2021; 1900 Federal Census; Ohio, U.S., Wills and Probate Records, 1786–1998, ancestry.com; Franz Fehr Death Card, Cincinnati Birth and Death Records, 1865–1912, DRC.

75. Find A Grave, "Barbara Maas," https://www.findagrave.com/memorial /152585189/barbara-maas, and "Bertha Springman," https://www. findagrave.com/memorial/173926862/bertha-springman; 1900 Federal Census, ancestry.com.

76. "Cincinnati Woman Commits Suicide in Toledo Hotel by Cutting Wrists," *Cincinnati Enquirer*, September 13, 1903; Deed Index Book, Series 6, Book 28, page 4, Hamilton County Recorder's Office; Ohio Deaths, 1908–53, familysearch.org.

77. Cincinnati Better Housing League, *A Tenement House Survey in Cincinnati* (Cincinnati, OH: Better Housing League, 1921), 4–5.

78. "Real Estate and Building," *Cincinnati Enquirer*, June 25, 1914.

79. Miller, *Boss Cox's Cincinnati*, 6–13; Cincinnati Better Housing League, *Tenement House Survey*, 2; "Small Sleeping Room…43 Elder," *Cincinnati Enquirer*, March 7, 1881; "65 Elder," *Cincinnati Enquirer*, November 10, 1882.

80. "A Sale of Real Estate," *Cincinnati Enquirer*, June 29, 1896.

81. "Friendly Findlay Market Folk Reverse Modern City Business Trend," *Cincinnati Post*, January 3, 1953.

82. Cincinnati Better Housing League, *Tenement House Survey in Cincinnati*, 7–9.

83. Ibid., 11.

84. Ibid., 4–5, 7.

85. Stradling, *Cincinnati*, 96.

86. Cincinnati Better Housing League, *Tenement House Survey in Cincinnati*, 7, 12.

87. Jayne Merkel, "New Marketplace Does It Better," *Cincinnati Enquirer*, May 31, 1981; "Markets," *Cincinnati Enquirer*, August 20, 1901; "Board of Health," *Cincinnati Enquirer*, December 22, 1910; "Oyster Dealers Fined," *Cincinnati Post*, March 15, 1917.

88. "Profiteering Charged in Complaint," *Cincinnati Enquirer*, December 11, 1923.

89. Stern, "Findlay Market and Over-the-Rhine Revisited," 43; Tilton, *Cincinnati's Historic Findlay Market*, 71.

90. Daniels, *Coming to America*, 159.

Chapter 3

91. Harry Mayo, "Eleven Hurt; Two Buildings Are Wrecked," *Cincinnati Post*, December 17, 1940; Dick Williams, "Volunteer Worker Seeks Kin in Debris, Tells of Mother's Scream After Blast," *Cincinnati Post*, December

17, 1940; "Chaos Greets 2 Patrolmen First on Scene," *Cincinnati Post*, December 17, 1940.

92. Hamilton County Ownership Card, Hamilton County Auditor; Williams' City Directories.

93. "Last Victim of Blast Is Found," *Cincinnati Post*, December 19, 1940; "Blast Takes 13 Lives; One Still Missing," *Cincinnati Enquirer*, December 18, 1940; Charles Bentrop, "Sure Mate's Body Lies in Wreckage of Blast," *Cincinnati Post*, December 18, 1940.

94. Stradling, *Cincinnati*, 125, 134; Miller and Tucker, *Changing Plans for America's Inner Cities*, xix.

95. "Old-Timers Aghast at Thought of Findlay Market's Fade-Out," *Cincinnati Post*, April 21, 1956.

96. Michael D. Morgan, *Over-the-Rhine: When Beer Was King* (Charleston, SC: The History Press, 2010), 149–50.

97. Williams' City Directories; 1900, 1920 Federal Censuses, ancestry.com; "Chris Sachs Summoned by Death," *Cincinnati Free Press*, December 23, 1938.

98. "Tabar Held to Jury," *Cincinnati Enquirer*, February 6, 1920; "George Tabar," *Cincinnati Enquirer*, May 22, 1920; "Café Owner Is Sentenced to Jail," *Cincinnati Enquirer*, November 28, 1923; Stradling, *Cincinnati*, 59.

99. John E. Porter, Superintendent of Public Maintenance, "Dear Mr. Root," May 2, 1938, Charles P. Taft II Papers, MSS 562, Box 61, Folder 6, CMC; Williams' City Directories; Stradling, *Cincinnati*, 103–4.

100. Williams' City Directories.

101. Zane L. Miller and Bruce Tucker, "The New Urban Politics: Planning and Development in Cincinnati, 1954–1988," in *Snowbelt Cities: Metropolitan Politics in the Northeast and Midwest Since World War II*, ed. Richard M. Bernard (Bloomington: Indiana University Press, 1990), 93–99.

102. City of Cincinnati, "Agreement for Occupancy of Market Stands," Charles P. Taft II Papers, MSS 562, Box 61, Folder 6, CMC.

103. "New Market Opens Here Saturday," *Cincinnati Post*, April 8, 1960; "Lower Market Group Irked," *Cincinnati Post*, February 26, 1929; "Stands to Be Torn Down for X-Way Access," *Cincinnati Post*, December 31, 1959; "Sixth-Street Market Stand Owners Appeal for a Place to Move," *Cincinnati Post*, September 25, 1959.

104. "Protest Explained Away," *Cincinnati Enquirer*, June 16, 1931; Cincinnati Views, "Markets," http://www.cincinnativiews.net/odds_&_ends_page_2.htm; C.O. Sherrill, City Manager, "Dear Sirs," April 6, 1938, Charles P. Taft II Papers, MSS 562, Box 61, Folder 6, CMC.

105. Findlay Market, "A Brief History," https://www.findlaymarket.org/ history; Tangiers, *Movable Markets*, 178.

106. Charles E. De Leuw, *Cincinnati Parking Studies: Neighborhood Business Districts, Findlay Market, Northside, Peebles Corner, Oakley, Hyde Park, Corryville, Mt. Washington, Pleasant Ridge*, vol. 1 (Chicago: Charles E. De Leuw, 1958); Calhoun, *Wholesale Fruit and Vegetable Market*, 13, 19; Saxon D. Clark, "Wholesale Produce Market Study," published by the City Planning Commission of Cincinnati, 1958, CMC.

107. Quoted in Miller and Tucker, *Changing Plans for America's Inner Cities*, 21; Eleanor Bell, "Open-Air Markets Still Lure Many Cincinnatians," *Cincinnati Post*, June 10, 1964.

108. "Old-Timers Aghast"; De Leuw, *Cincinnati Parking Studies*, vol. 2 (Chicago: Charles E. De Leuw, 1958), 1–1.

109. Stradling, *Cincinnati*, 113, 129.

110. "Construction of Viaduct Sought," *Cincinnati Enquirer*, December 13, 1934.

111. Frederick Yeiser, "Findlay Market," *Cincinnati Enquirer*, February 24, 1957.

112. Erika A. Lee, "The Chinese Exclusion Example: Race, Immigration, and American Gatekeeping, 1882–1924," *Journal of American Ethnic History* 21, no. 3 (Spring 2002): 36–62.

113. Hamilton County Ownership Card, Hamilton County Auditor; Williams' City Directories; 1900, 1910 and 1920 Federal Censuses, ancestry.com.

114. Stradling, *Cincinnati*, 123.

115. Hamilton County Ownership Card, Hamilton County Auditor; Williams' City Directories; 1920, 1930 and 1940 Federal Censuses, ancestry.com; Find A Grave, "Evelyn F. Manis," https://www.findagrave. com/memorial/78988936/evelyn-f-manis; ancestry.com, "Floyd Manis," https://search.ancestry.com/cgi-bin/sse.dll?dbid=60525&h=33451215 &indiv=try&o_vc=Record:OtherRecord&rhSource=61378.

116. Hamilton County Ownership Card, Hamilton County Auditor; Williams' City Directories; 1920, 1930 and 1940 Federal Censuses, ancestry.com; Find A Grave, "Evelyn F. Manis," https://www.findagrave. com/memorial/78988936/evelyn-f-manis; ancestry.com, "Floyd Manis."

117. Roger Daniels, *Guarding the Golden Door: American Immigration Policy and Immigrants Since 1882* (New York: Hill and Wang, 2004), 98, 102, 109.

118. Williams' City Directories; 1910, 1920, 1930 and 1940 Federal Censuses, ancestry.com.

119. "12 Refugees Due to Land," *Cincinnati Enquirer*, November 18, 1955.

120. "Refugees on Ship; To Land Relatives of Cincinnati Man," *Cincinnati Enquirer*, September 7, 1956; "Osi Begins Deportation Hearings Against Former Auschwitz Guard," *Jewish Telegraphic Agency*, January 18, 1989.

121. "Fugitive from Russian Work Camp Lands in U.S. En Route to Home in Cincinnati," *Cincinnati Enquirer*, November 11, 1947; "Girl Slave Laborer Tells of Flight to U.S.," *Syracuse Herald-Journal*, November 17, 1947.

122. Market Analysis, Sales Projections and Development Strategy for the Findlay Market Area in Cincinnati, Ohio," January 1984, III–9, Friends of Findlay Market Committee, US 88-44, Box 1, Folder Market Analysis, Sales Projections and Development Strategy, 1984, Blegen Library (hereafter BL), University of Cincinnati, Cincinnati, Ohio.

123. "Maytag," *Cincinnati Enquirer*, December 8, 1925; 1940 Williams' City Directory.

124. Williams' City Directories.

125. Williams' City Directories; 1900, 1920 and 1930 Federal Censuses, ancestry.com; ancestry.com, "George H. Leugers," https://search.ancestry.com/cgi-bin/sse.dll?indiv=1&dbid=60525&h=124973832&tid=&pid=&queryId=eeaf394cb81d0c218a0350f4ca802bc7&usePUB=true&_phsrc=xeC241&_phstart=successSource.

126. Create Your Jewish Legacy, "Alvin Bunny Meisel," http://createyourjewishlegacy.org/?pageID=1004.

127. 1920 Federal Census, ancestry.com; Find A Grave, "Sol Levine," https://www.findagrave.com/memorial/70658055/sol-levine.

128. "Harry Solway, 58, Dies; Veteran Furniture Dealer," *Cincinnati Enquirer*, August 5, 1956; Find A Grave, "Harry Solway," https://www.findagrave.com/memorial/5468643/harry-solway; 1920 Federal Census, ancestry.com; Hamilton County Ownership Card, Hamilton County Auditor.

129. 1900, 1910 and 1920 Federal Censuses, ancestry.com; Williams' City Directories; Bowdeya Tweh, "Leader Furniture Owners on Store Closing: 'We're Both Ready,'" *Cincinnati Enquirer*, November 28, 2016.

130. Williams' City Directories; Joseph B. Hall, "Barney Builds a Business," *Cincinnati Historical Society Bulletin* 26, no. 4 (October 1968): 290–316.

131. "Largest Unit in City," *Cincinnati Enquirer*, May 24, 1934; Friends of Findlay Market, "Key Improvements Needed for Market Survival," *Findlay Flyer*, December 1984, Friends of Findlay Market Committee, US 88-44, Box 1, Folder Pamphlets, BL; "Market Analysis, Sales Projections, and Development Strategy for the Findlay Market Area in Cincinnati, Ohio," January 1984, I–3, Friends of Findlay Market Committee, US 88-

44, Box 1, Folder Market Analysis, Sales Projections, and Development Strategy, 1984, BL.

132. Marc Levinson, *The Great A&P and the Struggle for Small Business in America* (New York: Hill and Wang, 2011), 13–22, 62.

133. Ibid., 8.

134. "Fifty Thousand Items," *Cincinnati Enquirer*, May 26, 1950.

135. Mickey deVisé and Kevin Luken, "Findlay Market Opening Day Parade: Statement of Significance," in "Ohio Historical Markers Application to the Ohio History Connection," June 30, 2019, CMC.

136. "Findlay Market Group Marches to Park for 20th Year to Open Baseball Season," *Cincinnati Post*, April 16, 1951; Richard Miller and Gregory L. Rhodes, "The Life and Times of Old Cincinnati Ballparks," *Queen City Heritage* 46, no. 2 (Summer 1988): 25–41.

Chapter 4

137. "Surrenders on NAACP Complaint," *Cincinnati Enquirer*, August 21, 1960.

138. "Market Analysis, Sales Projections, and Development Strategy," January 1984, I–2, Friends of Findlay Market Committee, US 88-44, Box 1, Folder Market Analysis, Sales Projections, and Development Strategy, 1984, BL; Cincinnati Planning Department, "Over-the-Rhine Comprehensive Plan Summary Report," 1984, 5, Friends of Findlay Market Committee, US 88-44, Box 1, Folder Over-the-Rhine Comprehensive Plan 1984 Summary Report, 1974, BL.

139. Miller and Tucker, *Changing Plans for America's Inner Cities*, xix; Keeanga-Yamahtta Taylor, *Race for Profit: How Banks and the Real Estate Industry Undermined Black Homeownership* (Chapel Hill: University of North Carolina Press, 2019), 226.

140. Miller and Tucker, *Changing Plans for America's Inner Cities*, xix; "Over-the-Rhine Today," *Cincinnati Enquirer*, July 16, 1995.

141. "Market Analysis, Sales Projections, and Development Strategy for the Findlay Market Area in Cincinnati, Ohio," January 1984, III–9, Friends of Findlay Market Committee, US 88-44, Box 1, Folder Market Analysis, Sales Projections, and Development Strategy, 1984, BL.

142. Williams' City Directories.

143. Carrie Blackmore Smith, "Dean's Mediterranean Imports Owner Kate Zaidan Leads a Spicy Life," *Cincinnati Magazine* (May 10, 2019).

144. Barbara Murphy, "Vietnam 'Boat' Family Starting New Life Here," *Cincinnati Enquirer*, October 23, 1979; Tilton, *Cincinnati's Historic Findlay Market*, 52.

145. Building Ownership Cards and Transfer Data, Hamilton County Auditor; Find A Grave; Philip G. Ciafardini and Pamela Ciafardini Casebolt, *Italians of Greater Cincinnati* (Charleston, SC: Arcadia Publishing, 2008), 81–82.

146. "Northern Liberties," *Cincinnati Enquirer*, August 20, 1941; Building Ownership Cards and Transfer Data, Hamilton County Auditor.

147. Building Ownership Cards and Transfer Data, Hamilton County Auditor; 1900, 1910, 1920, 1930 and 1940 Federal Censuses, ancestry.com; Find A Grave.

148. Building Ownership Cards and Transfer Data, Hamilton County Auditor.

149. Tilton, *Cincinnati's Historic Findlay Market*, 45.

150. "Findlay Market No Longer Families' Closed Shop," *Cincinnati Enquirer*, July 20, 1977; "New Market Law," *Cincinnati Enquirer*, December 26, 1976; Ellen Schmitz, "Ol' Findlay Market Just Won't Be Quite the Same," *Cincinnati Post*, March 3, 1977.

151. Schmitz, "Ol' Findlay Market."

152. Doug Trapp, "The Fight for Over-the-Rhine," *City Beat*, December 13, 2001.

153. Lance Freeman, *A Haven and a Hell: The Ghetto in Black America* (New York: Columbia University Press, 2019), 100.

154. Stradling, *Cincinnati*, 110.

155. Taylor, *Race for Profit*, 39; Robert M. Fogelson, *Bourgeois Nightmares: Suburbia, 1870–1930* (New Haven, CT: Yale University Press, 2005), 203.

156. Richard Rothstein, *The Color of Law: A Forgotten History of How Our Government Segregated America* (New York: Liveright Publishing Corporation, 2017), 65–66; Cincinnati District Home Owners' Loan Corporation, map, 1935, the Ohio State University Libraries, https://library.osu.edu/documents/redlining-maps-ohio/maps/Cincinnati_map.JPG.

157. Miller and Tucker, *Changing Plans for America's Inner Cities*, xix; Alyssa Konermann, "25,737 People Lived in Kenyon-Barr When the City Razed It to the Ground," *Cincinnati Magazine* (February 10, 2017).

158. "City," *Cincinnati Post*, April 18, 1959; "City—Two Rooms," *Cincinnati Enquirer*, January 30, 1958; "City—White," *Cincinnati Enquirer*, August 12, 1958.

159. "City—Colored," *Cincinnati Enquirer*, July 1, 1961.

160. Gerald White, "Ohio Fair Housing Law Full of Loopholes," *Cincinnati Enquirer*, April 6, 1968; Freeman, *Haven and a Hell*, 127; Charles Casey-Leininger, "Going Home: The Struggle for Fair Housing in Cincinnati, 1900 to 2007," 2017, 10–13, https://homecincy.org/about-us; Mi Herzog, "HOME Has Moved from Pledges to Proof," *Cincinnati Enquirer*, August 10, 1980.

161. Miller and Tucker, *Changing Plans for America's Inner Cities*, 161; "City—Nr Findlay Market," *Cincinnati Post*, August 11, 1982.

162. See Taylor, *Race for Profit*.

163. Cliff Peale and Ken Alltucker, "Land Shifts for a Landlord," *Cincinnati Enquirer*, August 19, 2001.

164. Ibid.

165. Trapp, "Fight for Over-the-Rhine."

166. Chris Wetterich, "How Has OTR's Housing Been Transformed Over the Years? The Stats May Surprise You," *Cincinnati Business Courier*, January 28, 2016.

167. "Six Sentenced in Illicit Resale of Food Stamps," *Cincinnati Post*, December 13, 1977.

168. Gary Sullivan, "A&P to Shut Down Last Stores in Area," *Cincinnati Enquirer*, December 20, 1978; "Cookie Vogelpohl: Founder of Our Daily Bread, OTR Soup Kitchen, Dies at 75," *WCPO News*, December 18, 2016.

169. Mark Curnutte and Cameron McWhirter, "Over-the-Rhine: Two Sides to Revitalization," *Cincinnati Enquirer*, July 16, 1995; Max Ash, "Dear Mr. Luken," July 2, 1985, Marian A. Spencer Papers, MSS 888, Box 16, Folder Findlay Market 1983–85, CMC.

170. Ken Wilson, "Lead Poison Forces Family to Move," *Cincinnati Post*, November 24, 1988; Len Penix, "Apartment Owner Blames City for Lead Poisoning of Toddler," *Cincinnati Post*, November 26, 1988.

171. "Girl, 2, Is Killed in Fire, Brother Critically Burned," *Cincinnati Post*, January 4, 1968; "Two Youngsters Died in Elder Street Fire," *Cincinnati Enquirer*, January 5, 1968; "Vacant Building Blaze Injures 3 Firefighters," *Cincinnati Enquirer*, October 18, 1995.

172. "Over-the-Rhine Today," *Cincinnati Enquirer*, July 16, 1995; Tanya Bricking, "Findlay to Fight Crime," *Cincinnati Enquirer*, May 12, 1999.

173. Tanya Bricking, "Police Shut Down Elder Café," *Cincinnati Enquirer*, February 26, 1999; Lisa Donovan and Perry Brothers, "Judge Orders Elder Café to Remain Padlocked," *Cincinnati Enquirer*, March 19, 1999.

174. Lew Moores, "The Day Before the Big Day at Findlay Market," *Cincinnati Post*, November 27, 1981; "Woman Bound to Grand Jury," *Cincinnati Post*, July 21, 1970; "70-Year-Old Woman Held in Café Shooting," *Cincinnati Post*, April 12, 1974; Hal Metzger, "Young Witness Says She Saw Dixon Beat Vearelene Jackson," *Cincinnati Post*, September 8, 1976; "Dixon Found Guilty," *Cincinnati Enquirer*, September 16, 1976; "Man Is Charged in Shooting Death," *Cincinnati Post*, October 13, 1980; Al Andry, "New Landlord Orders Bar to Move Out," *Cincinnati Post*, July 31, 1984; Richard Gibeau, "Sentence Imposed on 4 in Food Stamp Swindle," *Cincinnati Post*, November 15, 1977.

175. Freeman, *Haven and a Hell*, 189; Carol Anderson, *White Rage: The Unspoken Truth of Our Racial Divide* (New York: Bloomsbury, 2016), 136.

176. Stradling, *Cincinnati*, 138–39.

177. Ibid., 151.

Chapter 5

178. Urban Marketing Collaborative Inc. (hereafter UMC), *Findlay Market Master Business Development Plan* (1995), 8.

179. Crocker, "Findlay Market's Bounty," *Cincinnati Magazine* (October 2003); "Findlay Market: 150 Years of Supplying Cincinnati," *Cincinnati Enquirer*, October 6, 2002.

180. "Alley: Widening Stretches into a 5-Year Project," *Cincinnati Enquirer*, December 27, 1999.

181. Lizabeth Cohen, *Saving America's Cities: Ed Logue and the Struggle to Renew Urban America in the Suburban Age* (New York: Farrar, Straus, and Giroux, 2019), 100–101. See also David Stradling and Richard Stradling, *Where the River Burned: Carl Stokes and the Struggle to Save Cleveland* (Ithaca, NY: Cornell University Press, 2015).

182. Miller and Tucker, "New Urban Politics," 93–99.

183. Miller and Tucker, *Changing Plans for America's Inner Cities*, 73.

184. "Old Findlay Market Off to a Fresh Start," *Cincinnati Post*, June 10, 1974; Tilton, *Cincinnati's Historic Findlay Market*, 84–88.

185. Friends of Findlay Market, "Findlay Market and the Community Center Dedication Day, Sunday, June 9, 1974," 34–41, Friends of Findlay Market Committee, US 88-44, Box 1, Folder Findlay Market Dedication Day and the Community Center, 1974, BL.

186. Sharon Maloney and Jane Blazes, "Brush Asks for Aid for Failing Findlay Market," *Cincinnati Post*, December 15, 1978.

187. Friends of Findlay Market, "Findlay Market and the Community Center Dedication Day," 31; Miller and Tucker, *Changing Plans for America's Inner Cities*, 111–15.

188. Freeman, *Haven and a Hell*, 133–42.

189. Sanford A. Youkilis, Senior City Planner, "Report and Recommendation on a Proposed Change of Zoning to Establish Interim Development Control (ICD) District No. 3 in the Vicinity of Findlay Market," April 22, 1975, Charles P. Taft II Papers, 1922–1977, MSS 562, Box 51, Folder 1, City Council Papers—Findlay Market Area, 1972–1975, CMC; Miller and Tucker, *Changing Plans for America's Inner Cities*, 99–100, 136–37.

190. Cincinnati Planning Department, "Over-the-Rhine Comprehensive Plan Summary Report," 1984, 6, Friends of Findlay Market Committee, US 88-44, Box 1, Folder Over-the-Rhine Comprehensive Plan 1984 Summary Report, 1974, BL.

191. Miller and Tucker, *Changing Plans for America's Inner Cities*, 161.

192. Mark Curnutte and Cameron McWhirter, "Over-the-Rhine: Two Sides to Revitalization," *Cincinnati Enquirer*, July 16, 1995.

193. Wayne Chapman, Director of Neighborhood Housing and Conservation, "Members of City Council—Ordinance and Agreement with Invest in Neighborhoods," January 5, 1994; City Council, Ordinance No. 110-1997, April 23, 1997, City of Cincinnati Digitized City Council Records (hereafter CC); Dave Krieger, "City Prepares 'Anti-Displacement Law' for Poor," *Cincinnati Enquirer*, May 21, 1980.

194. Curnutte and McWhirter, "Over-the-Rhine"; "OTR: Some Developers Turning It into Place to Be," *Cincinnati Enquirer*, February 1, 1998.

195. Urban Design Associates, "Central Riverfront Urban Design Master Plan," April 2000, https://www.cincinnati-oh.gov/cityofcincinnati/linkservid/E506D20A-9B46-F3A6-6D763ECBC854F106/showMeta/0; Reed Albergotti and Cameron McWhirter, "A Stadium's Costly Legacy Throws Taxpayers for a Loss," *Wall Street Journal*, July 12, 2011; Darrell Preston, "Cincinnati's Worst Stadium Deal Ever Seeks Lower Borrowing Costs," *Bloomberg*, July 28, 2016.

196. "3CDC: New Deal Maker," *Cincinnati Enquirer*, July 2, 2003; Colin Woodard, "How Cincinnati Salvaged the Nation's Most Dangerous Neighborhood," *Politico Magazine* (June 16, 2016).

197. John Cranley, "Motion 200205272," May 30, 2002, CC; Milton Dohoney Jr., City Manager, "To Mayor and Members of City Council—Community Development Spring/Summer 2008 NOFA Projects," September 15, 2008, CC; Dan Monk, "Razing the Roof: Some Laud Developer for His Action, While Others Simply Bristle," *Cincinnati Business Courier*, January 6, 2003; David E. Rager, City Manager, "To Mayor and Members of City Council—Communication Concerning the Manufacturing District Designation in Over-the-Rhine," December 14, 2005, CC; Mark Curnutte, "Lower Price Hill Getting Makeover Times Two," *Cincinnati Enquirer*, March 1, 2016.

198. Curnutte and McWhirter, "Over-the-Rhine."

199. City Council, Ordinance No. E/70-1996, April 24, 1996, CC.

200. Colman Andrews, "A Food Lover's Dream in the Heart of Seattle," *Metropolitan Home*, September 1984; Pike Place Market, "History," http:// pikeplacemarket.org/history.

201. Jane Prendergast, "It May Be a Market in Decline," *Cincinnati Enquirer*, December 16, 1993; "Market Analysis, Sales Projections, and Development Strategy for the Findlay Market Area in Cincinnati, Ohio," January 1984, III-6, Friends of Findlay Market Committee, US 88-44, Box 1, Folder Market Analysis, Sales Projections, and Development Strategy, 1984, BL.

202. UMC, *Findlay Market Master Business Development Plan*, 4.

203. Mary Beth Crocker, "Findlay Market's Bounty," *Cincinnati Magazine* (October 2003); James L. Mackie, "Dear Ms. Spencer," July 16, 1985, Marian A. Spencer Papers, MSS 888, Box 16, Folder Findlay Market 1983–85, CMC.

204. Cincinnati Board of Park Commissioners, Meeting Minutes, March 21, 1996, Cincinnati Park Board Records, Bettman Nature Preserve, Cincinnati, Ohio.

205. UMC, *Findlay Market Master Business Development Plan*, 72, 19.

206. City Council, Ordinance No. E/70-1996, April 24, 1996; Evonne L. Kovach, Director of Economic Development, "To Mayor and Members of City Council—Resolution of Intent to Appropriate 115 West Elder Street, Findlay Market," May 16, 2001; City Council, Ordinance No. 85-2001, June 27, 2001, CC.

207. City Council, Ordinance No. 354-1996, November 6, 1996, CC; Glaser Associates, *Findlay Market Revitalization: Phase 2/Bid Package 2, North Buildings Renovation* (drawing no. D202), construction drawing, August 11, 1997.

208. Jim Tarbell, Councilmember, "Motion," November 21, 2001; William V. Langevin, Director of Buildings and Inspections, "To Mayor and Members of City Council—1721–1725 Vine Street," January 24, 2000, CC; "Saving a Face (And a Back Wall)," *Cincinnati Enquirer*, January 23, 2004.

209. Interview with Beth Johnson, urban conservator, March 9, 2020.

210. Timothy H. Riordan, Finance Director, "To Mayor and Members of Council—Emergency Ordinance—Findlay Market North Addition Repairs," June 13, 2001; City Council, Ordinance No. 195-2001, June 20, 2001; City Council, Ordinance No. 275-2001, September 6, 2001, CC; Tilton, *Cincinnati's Historic Findlay Market*, 110–12; Susan Vela, "Findlay Market Takes a Step Forward," *Cincinnati Enquirer*, April 22, 2001.

211. Tom Jackson, Market Manager, "To Members of the Findlay Market Network Planning Committee," January 26, 1999, Bobbie Sterne Papers, US 07-06, Box 5, Folder 1999, BL.

212. Valerie A. Lemmie, City Manager, "To Mayor and Members of Council—Ordinance—Findlay Market Lease and Management Agreement," June 30, 2004; Robert J. Pickford, Executive Director, CFFM, "Findlay Market Revitalization Business Development Phase," May 2004, CC.

213. UMC, *Findlay Market Master Business Development Plan*, 24; City Council, Ordinance No. R/132, October 9, 1996; Ordinance No. 281-1996, September 11, 1996; Ordinance No. 109, April 5, 1995; Ordinance No. 275-2001, September 6, 2001; Ordinance No. 300—2000, August 2, 2000, CC.

214. H.C. Niehoff, President, Board of Trustees, CFFM, "Dear Council Members Reece, Cole, and Smitherman," June 25, 2004, city report, CC; Valerie A. Lemmie, City Manager, "Vendor Diversity at Findlay Market," April 13, 2005, CC.

215. Findlay Kitchen, "About Findlay Kitchen," https://findlaykitchen.org/whoweare; Joe Hansbauer, President and CEO, CFFM, "The Findlay Market Kitchen," presentation, February 2014; City Council, Ordinance No. 211-2018, June 27, 2018, CC.

216. Findlay Market, "SNAP Plus, Produce Perks, & EBT Resources," https://www.findlaymarket.org/snapproduceperksebt.

217. Mary Beth Crocker, "Findlay Market's Bounty," *Cincinnati Magazine* (October 2003).

218. City Council, Ordinance No. 180-2014, June 25, 2014; City of Cincinnati, "Preferred Developer Agreement—OTR Holdings Inc.," June 25, 2014; Ordinance No. 119-2018; City Council, "Emergency Ordinance-2014," September 24, 2014, CC.

219. Community Building Institute, *2015 Housing Inventory of OTR and Pendleton* (Cincinnati, OH: Xavier University, 2016).

220. Ibid.

221. U.S. Census Bureau, "Population Estimates, July 1, 2019 (V2019)—Cincinnati, Ohio," Quick Facts, https://www.census.gov/quickfacts/cincinnaticityohio; Chris Wetterich, "Takeaways from the 2020 Census and OTR's Mysterious Population Decline," *Cincinnati Business Courier*, August 13, 2021.

ABOUT THE AUTHOR

Alyssa McClanahan is an independent writer and scholar who loves cities. She received her PhD in history from the University of Cincinnati and has worked as a historian and historic preservationist for many years in downtown Cincinnati.

Visit us at
www.historypress.com

CPSIA information can be obtained
at www.ICGtesting.com
Printed in the USA
BVHW042259091221
623628BV00011B/3

9 781540 250483